通用学术英语系列教材

学术英语听说交流
中 级

主编
赵 燚 杨朝春

编者
田 园

清华大学出版社
北京

内 容 简 介

本教材立足全球胜任力培养需求，以提高学生英语听说交流的实际应用能力为目标，在充分借鉴和吸收国内外教学理论和方法的基础上，考虑中国学习者在英语听说方面的共性问题，设计循序渐进的听说策略以及输入输出相结合的语言任务。全书按照内容分为四大主题：学术生活、心理健康、语言和领导力。每个主题包括两个教学单元，单元构架体现以"听"促"说"，依据听力材料规划听力理解策略、口语交流及语音微技能等，最终实现教学目标。

本教材适用对象是英语能力达到《大学英语教学指南》（2020 版）中"提高目标"的学生，或水平相当的英语学习者。教材另配有 PPT 电子课件和参考答案，读者可登录 www.tsinghuaelt.com 下载使用。

版权所有，侵权必究。举报：010-62782989，beiqinquan@tup.tsinghua.edu.cn。

图书在版编目（CIP）数据

学术英语听说交流：中级 / 赵燚，杨朝春主编．
北京：清华大学出版社，2024.7. --（通用学术英语系列教材）. --ISBN 978-7-302-66608-0

Ⅰ. H319.9

中国国家版本馆 CIP 数据核字第 20249BS147 号

责任编辑：刘 艳
封面设计：李伯骥
责任校对：王凤芝
责任印制：刘 菲

出版发行：清华大学出版社
网　　址：https://www.tup.com.cn, https://www.wqxuetang.com
地　　址：北京清华大学学研大厦 A 座　　　　**邮　编**：100084
社 总 机：010-83470000　　　　　　　　　　**邮　购**：010-62786544
投稿与读者服务：010-62776969, c-service@tup.tsinghua.edu.cn
质量反馈：010-62772015, zhiliang@tup.tsinghua.edu.cn
印 装 者：三河市少明印务有限公司
经　　销：全国新华书店
开　　本：185mm×260mm　　　　**印　张**：10　　　　**字　数**：234 千字
版　　次：2024 年 8 月第 1 版　　　　　　　　　**印　次**：2024 年 8 月第 1 次印刷
定　　价：49.00 元

产品编号：099031-01

在全球化进程不断深化的背景下，大学英语教学承载着培养具备国际视野和精准国际传播能力的高素质人才的重要使命。教育部颁布的《大学英语教学指南》（2020版）明确指出："大学英语在巩固学生通用英语能力的同时，应进一步强化其学术英语交流能力和跨文化交际能力。"

为了全面落实指南的要求，并进一步满足新时代大学生英语学习的实际需求，清华大学语言教学中心团队从国家与社会的要求、外语教与学的理论以及外语学习者的成长特点三个视角综合考量，精心研发了"通用学术英语系列教材"，旨在为学生提供全面而深入的学术英语教育，进而提高他们的英语学术素养和国际学术交流能力。

本系列教材分为听说和读写两大模块，包括《学术英语听说交流（中级）》《学术英语听说交流（高级）》《学术英语议论文阅读与写作》和《学术英语研究论文阅读与写作》四个分册。其中，《学术英语听说交流（中级）》和《学术英语听说交流（高级）》聚焦学术环境中的听说技能，通过模拟真实的学术交流场景，帮助学生增强国际学术交流能力；《学术英语议论文阅读与写作》和《学术英语研究论文阅读与写作》围绕高等教育中最常用的两种学术语体提供了丰富的阅读材料和写作指导，旨在提升学生的学术英语阅读和写作能力。

本系列教材具有如下特点：

- **需求导向：** 紧密契合新时代对人才培养的新要求，特别是对学术英语能力的要求，与《大学英语教学指南》（2020版）中提出的提高目标和发展目标相对应。
- **理论指导：** 基于外语教与学的理论，贯彻以学生学习为中心，以产出应用为导向的教学理念。

- **实践转化：** 将理论融于实践，通过系统化的学习和训练，聚焦语言应用，从而提升学生的综合素养，并顺利实现从通用英语到学术英语的过渡。

- **能力提升：** 专注于提高学生的学术素养，助力专业学习，确保学生能够熟练运用英语进行学术交流和开展研究。

我们坚信，通过本系列教材的学习，学生不仅能够实现从通用英语到学术英语的过渡，更能在全球化的广阔舞台上，增强自身的学术竞争力，同时培养出独立思考、批判性分析、创新解决问题的能力以及学术责任感。

感谢清华大学本科教育教学改革项目的支持，感谢清华大学语言教学中心的大力协助，以及所有参与本系列教材编写、审校和出版工作的同仁们的辛勤付出。愿本系列教材能够成为学生通往学术英语领域的桥梁，助力他们在国际舞台上绽放光彩。

总主编

2024 年 7 月于清华园

《学术英语听说交流（中级）》作为"通用学术英语系列教材"中的一本，秉承清华大学"三位一体"的教育理念——价值塑造、能力培养和知识传授，致力于提升学生的全球胜任力，特别是英语听说交流的实际应用能力，并同步培养批判性思维能力和学术素养，以增强学生在国际交流中的沟通效能。

一、教材适用对象

本教材适用对象是英语能力达到《大学英语教学指南》（2020版）中"提高目标"要求的学生，或水平相当的英语学习者。通过本教材的学习，学生将系统地掌握和应用基础语音知识及听说策略，提升抓取英语视听信息的能力，并流畅地运用英语陈述和交流学术观点。教材内容和安排适合一个学期的完整教学，确保学生在有限的时间内有效地掌握并运用所学知识。

二、教材特点

本教材以解决大学英语听说教学中的实际问题为出发点，借鉴并融合了国内外的教学理论与方法，通过单元项目设计，提供了循序渐进的听说学习策略和输入输出相结合的语言任务。教材主要特色如下：

1. **真实性与实用性**：教材选用的音视频均为真实、规范的现代英语，时长为10分钟左右的访谈、微型讲座或学术演讲。结合单元主题及教学重点，教材设计了语音微技能板块，将连读、失爆破、重音、语调等语音知识融入主题内容学习，以应对中国学习者在听力理解和口语表达中常见的语音混淆、辨词障碍、连读不畅等问题。语音练习材料的原文均由清华大学语言教学中心的外籍教师编写，呈现真实的交流场景，旨在提升学生语音表达准确性和口语流畅性的同时，帮助他们熟悉和掌握实用的主题场景用语，为今后的学术和职业发展打下坚实基础。

2. **趣味性与思辨性**：教材主题贴近学生生活，旨在激发研讨兴趣，提供新颖的视角，引发问题意识和批判性思维；同时，鼓励学生收集翔实的证据来支撑观点，培养学术意识，增强跨文化理解力，通过强调口语表达的逻辑性、流畅度和内容深度，全面提升英语沟通能力。教材在听说练习中设计了以主题内容为依托的分析性、细节性和批判性问题，注重引导学生学用结合，开展基于现实问题的团队合作探究，旨在通过多维学习方式激发学生的学习主动性，更深入地理解和应用语言，实现形式、意义、语用的有机结合。

3. **系统性与拓展性**：教材注重培养学生的英语学习与应用习惯，循序渐进地提升英语听说能力，增强英语交流信心。每个单元的结构设计以"听"促"说"，并基于听力内容难度和教学重难点，提供一系列听力理解策略指导。同时，听力练习为口语活动提供有效的语言输入，全书口语交流策略的编写从对听力材料的复述、概括、评价，逐步过渡到自主组织演讲、会话互动及话轮转换，帮助学生稳步夯实口语表达基础。此外，教材每个单元最后还提供了 3~5 个主题拓展视听资源，学生可依据内容和难度选择并自主学习，也可作为教学测试资源使用。

三、内容安排

本教材按照内容分为四大主题：学术生活（Academic Life）、心理健康（Psychological Health）、语言（Language）和领导力（Leadership）。每个主题包含两个教学单元。每个单元围绕两个主要听力材料设计了导入讨论（Lead-in）、教学目标（Learning Objectives）、核心听力理解策略（Listening Focus）、口语交流策略（Speech Workshop）和语音微技能（Pronunciation Workshop）等板块。这样的结构安排既提供了清晰的学习路径，也能逐步增加学生的学习挑战度和获得感。

前言

本教材是清华大学语言教学中心"英语听说交流（B）"课程教学团队多年教学科研实践的结晶。感谢教学团队中三位外籍教师［英］Adam Rose、［美］Christina Yun 和［澳］John Paul Grima 提供源自真实语境的语音练习材料。感谢清华大学本科教育教学改革项目的支持以及所有参与本教材编写、审校和出版的专家学者和工作人员。由于时间紧迫，书中如有疏漏或不当之处，恳请读者不吝赐教，提出宝贵意见，以促使我们在未来的教学中不断改进和完善教材内容。

编者

2024 年 7 月于清华园

CONTENTS

Themes	Units	Academic Topics	Listening Focus	Listening Practice
Academic Life	Unit 1	Time Management 1	Dictation & Note-Taking 3	Section A: How to Study More Effectively? 4
	Unit 2	Doing Research 17	Grouping Related Items 19	Section A: The Scientific Method 20
Psychological Health	Unit 3	Happiness 33	Implied Meaning 35	Section A: Confucian Philosophy on Happiness 36
	Unit 4	Depression 53	Details 55	Section A: Understanding Depression—Symptoms, Causes & Treatments 55
Language	Unit 5	Language Learning 71	Signal Words 73	Section A: Why Is It Necessary to Learn a Foreign Language? 74
	Unit 6	Language History 91	Terms & Concepts 93	Section A: Language, Evolution's Great Mystery 94
Leadership	Unit 7	Teamwork 111	Comparison & Contrast 113	Section A: What Makes a Team? 115
	Unit 8	Motivation 129	Speaker's Intention & Attitude 131	Section A: Self-Managing Company 132

	Speech Workshop	Pronunciation Workshop
Section B: Inside the Mind of a Master Procrastinator 6	Retelling 12	Vowels 14
Section B: Ethics in Research 23	Summarizing 28	Consonants 30
Section B: What Makes a Good Life? Lessons from the Longest Study on Happiness 40	Reviewing 46	Liaison 48
Section B: Did I Inherit Mental Illness? 60	Informative Speaking 63	Loss of Plosion 66
Section B: Learning a Language—Speak It like You're Playing a Video Game 79	Persuasive Speaking 83	Stress 86
Section B: The History of English 98	Delivering a Speech 104	Accent Variation 107
Section B: How to Turn a Group of Strangers into a Team? 118	Turn-Taking 122	Contractions of Auxiliary & Modal Verbs 124
Section B: How Your Brain Responds to Stories—and Why They Are Crucial for Leaders? 135	Seminar Discussion 139	Intonation 141

Unit 1

Time Management

1. *"A journey of a thousand miles begins with the first step."*
   —Lao Zi (late Spring and Autumn Period, the date of birth and death is unknown), ancient Chinese philosopher, thinker, writer, and historian, the founder and principal representative of the Taoist School

2. *"To choose time is to save time."*
   —Francis Bacon (1561–1626), English lawyer, statesman, essayist, historian, and philosopher

Lead-in

It is said that time is equal for everyone. To manage time well is the very first step to succeeding in academic life in college. However, college students often find it hard to allocate time. The following table is a one-day schedule of a top Tsinghua University student, which went viral online several years ago. What are your thoughts about this? How do you schedule a working day in college? Are you good at managing time? Please review the expressions from the Preparing to Speak box and use them in discussion with your classmates.

	Week 4—Tuesday			
Morning	6:00–6:40	6:40–8:00	8:00–9:35	9:35–11:25
	Get up; have breakfast	Review *Calculus 2*; do homework—*College Physics*	Read *Gone with the Wind*	Attend a lecture—*Calculus 2*
Noon	11:25–13:30			
	Have lunch; print course materials; have a noon break			
Afternoon	13:30–15:05	15:20–16:55	16:55–18:40	
	Have PE class	Attend a lecture—*History*	Have dinner; review *Calculus 2*	
Evening and late night	18:40–21:45	21:45–23:00	23:00–01:00	01:00–
	Attend a lecture—*Fiction*	Do homework; listen to *CNN*	Self-study	Sleep

Match the words and phrases with their definitions.

1. a tight schedule
2. assignment
3. deadline
4. leisure
5. short-term
6. long-term
7. pull an all-nighter
8. timetable

a. relating to a short period of time
b. (a plan showing) the subjects to be studied in a course
c. continuing for a long time into the future
d. spend all night doing something
e. the list of planned activities is under time pressure
f. a piece of work as part of one's studies or job
g. a time or day by which something must be done
h. based on clear thought and reason

Unit 1
Time Management

9. syllabus
10. rational

i. the time when you are not working or doing duties
j. a detailed plan showing when activities will happen

Learning Objectives

This unit will lead you to figure out the essentials of time management. Upon completion of this unit, you will be able to

√ apply expressions related to time management in discussing academic studies;

√ adopt word-by-word dictation and note-taking to improve listening accuracy;

√ identify and differentiate vowel sounds in pronunciation;

√ retell what you hear in an organized manner.

Listening Focus

Dictation & Note-Taking

Dictation means you write down what you hear word-by-word. It is a time-honored listening skill to raise your awareness of vocabulary, grammar, cohesive devices as well as punctuation. You may start with short recordings of one or two lines, and then transition to paragraph dictation. There are basically three steps to improving listening accuracy through dictation. First, listen to the recording for the main ideas. Second, type or write down exactly what you hear, paying attention to every detail such as pronunciation and spelling. Third, check your dictation against the answers and learn from your mistakes. This practice helps improve listening accuracy.

Different from dictation, **taking organized notes** is mostly used to get the gist of the listening material. When you listen, you may follow the outline of the speaker to catch both the main point and its supporting details. During this process, use critical thinking to separate important information from unimportant details. Although it is up to you to develop your style in note-taking, noting down the main point on the left side and its supporting details on the right is suggested. To do it efficiently, you may develop shorthand such as abbreviations for words (e.g., TM for *time management*) or symbols (e.g., & for *and*).

Listening Practice

Section A

Introduction to the listening material: This BBC talk illustrates how to study more effectively from the perspective of time management. Instead of listing tips, the presenter adopts an interactive way to draw the audience's attention to the importance of time allocation in achieving efficiency.

Glossary

Study the words and phrases in the glossary, especially the unfamiliar ones. Do you know how to pronounce or use them in sentences? Use a dictionary to find out more information if necessary.

Words

burst	n.	a sudden increase in something, especially for a short period（尤指短期的）突然增加；迸发
commitment	n.	something that you must do or deal with, and that takes your time 必须做（或处理）的事情
concentration	n.	the ability to think carefully about something you are doing and nothing else 专注，专心
childcare	n.	care for children provided by either the government, an organization, or a person, while parents are at work or are absent for another reason 儿童看护，儿童照管
desperate	adj.	very serious or bad 非常严重的；非常糟糕的
distraction	n.	something that prevents someone from giving his or her attention to something else 分心的事；分散注意力的东西
effectively	adv.	in a way that is successful and achieves what you want 有效地
flexible	adj.	able to change or be changed easily according to the situation 可变动的；灵活的；可变通的

Unit 1
Time Management

| procrastination | n. | the act of delaying something that must be done, often because it is unpleasant or boring（通常指因为无趣、没有意思而）拖延 |

Phrases

film a video	to record moving pictures with a camera 拍摄视频
hang on	to wait for a short time 稍等一会儿
switch off	to stop giving your attention to someone or something 不再关注，不再理睬

Task 1　Analytical Listening

Watch the video for the first time and complete the outline of the talk.

How to Study More Effectively?

	Main Ideas	Supporting Details/Examples
Questions	(1) _____	Work, family events, childcare, travel, etc.
	(2) _____	Pass the course? Get a specific grade?
	(3) _____	When? Where? With music? With coffee/chocolate?
Problems	Distraction (4) _____	(5) _____. Try working in (6) _____. (7) _____, e.g., "I can eat this lovely chocolate, but only after I finish reading this."

5

Task 2 Detailed Listening

Listen to the audio clips and fill in the blanks with the exact words or phrases you hear from the lecture.

1) _____ is just one thing we need to do.

2) Take a good look at the _____, exams and _____, and old exam papers to find out how much you need to do.

3) Take a good look at your _____: You might need to _____ some if you don't have enough time.

4) Try to do your most difficult tasks _____.

5) Even if you _____, you still need to be _____.

Task 3 Critical Listening

Watch the video again and discuss the following questions with your language partner.

1) Why does the presenter mention his Mum in the talk?

2) The presenter argues that any time plan should be flexible. To what extent do you think that we may manage our schedule flexibly?

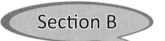

Section B

Introduction to the listening material: In this TED talk—"Inside the Mind of a Master Procrastinator", Tim Urban, a popular blog writer (blogger), has explained why people procrastinate in a metaphorical and inspiring way. According to Tim, we should think harder to shake the habit of waiting before running out of time.

Glossary

Study the words and phrases in the glossary, especially the unfamiliar ones. Do you know how to pronounce or use them in sentences? Use a dictionary to find out more information if necessary.

Unit 1 Time Management

Words

contain	*v.*	to control or hide a strong emotion, such as excitement or anger 克制，抑制，控制（情绪）
civilization	*n.*	human society with its well-developed social organizations, or the culture and way of life of a society or country at a particular period in time 文明社会；（特定时期特定社会或国家的）文明，文化
dive	*v.*	to move quickly, often in order to avoid something（为躲避而）冲，奔，扑
dormant	*adj.*	used to describe something that is not active or growing but has the ability to be active at a later time 蛰伏的；沉睡的，休眠的
dread	*n.*	a strong feeling of fear or worry 恐惧，害怕；忧虑
embarrassment	*n.*	the feeling of being embarrassed, or something that makes you feel embarrassed 尴尬，窘迫；局促不安；令人尴尬的事
entrepreneurial	*adj.*	having to do with the creation and development of economic ventures; of, relating to, characteristic of, or suited to an entrepreneur 企业家的；企业家精神的
ethic	*n.*	a system of accepted beliefs that control behavior, especially such a system based on morals 行为准则，伦理；（尤指）道德体系，道德规范
frustration	*n.*	the feeling of being annoyed or less confident because you cannot achieve what you want, or something that makes you feel like this（因不能满足需求而）沮丧；令人沮丧的事物
guardian	*n.*	someone who protects something 保护者，护卫者，维护者
hypothesis	*n.*	an idea or explanation for something that is based on known facts but has not yet been proved 假设，假说
insane	*adj.*	extremely unreasonable or stupid 疯狂的；荒唐的
intense	*adj.*	extreme and forceful or (of a feeling) very strong 强烈的；极度的

literally	*adv.*	used to emphasize what you are saying（用于强调所说的话）确实地，真正地
mayhem	*n.*	a situation in which there is little or no order or control 混乱状态
mechanism	*n.*	a way of doing something that is planned or part of a system 体制；结构方式
miraculously	*adv.*	in a way that is very surprising or difficult to believe 奇迹般地；不可思议地
momentum	*n.*	the force that keeps an object moving or keeps an event developing after it has started 动量，冲量；冲力；推动力；势头
motion	*n.*	the act or process of moving, or a particular action or movement 动；运动；移动
overlap	*n.*	the amount by which two things or activities cover the same area 重叠部分；相同之处
panic	*n.*	a sudden strong feeling of fear that prevents reasonable thought and action 恐慌，惊慌
perplex	*v.*	to confuse and worry someone slightly by being difficult to understand or solve 使困惑，使茫然；使担忧
procrastinator	*n.*	someone who keeps delaying things that must be done 拖延者，有拖延症的人
propagate	*v.*	(of a plant or animal) to produce young plants or animals（动植物）繁殖，繁衍
release	*v.*	to allow something to be shown in public or to be available for use 公开；公布；发布
self-hatred	*n.*	an extremely strong feeling of dislike for oneself 自我憎恨，憎恶
species	*n.*	a set of animals or plants in which the members have similar characteristics to each other and can breed with each other（动植物的）种，物种
sprint	*v.*	to run as fast as you can over a short distance, either in a race or because you are in a great hurry to get somewhere 短距离快速奔跑，冲刺

Unit 1 Time Management

tribal	*adj.*	relating to a tribe 部落的；部族的
visualize	*v.*	to form a picture of someone or something in your mind, in order to imagine or remember him, her, or it 使形象化；使能被看见

Phrases

be supposed to	to have to; to have a duty or a responsibility to 应该，应当
bump something up	to increase the amount or size of something 增加，提高（数量或尺寸）
for the sake of somebody	in order to help or bring advantage to someone 为了（某人）的利益；为了帮助（某人）
instant gratification	choosing something that is fun and easy instead of something challenging and important 即时满足
kick up or be in / go into high gear	to be or become very active, exciting, or productive 变得非常活跃或兴奋、高效
look down on somebody	to think that you are better than someone 看不起，小看，蔑视
lose one's mind	to become mentally ill, or to start behaving in a silly or strange way 精神失常；失去理智
make sense	to be clear and easy to understand 有意义，讲得通，言之有理
stay/be aware of	to know that something exists, or have knowledge or experience of a particular thing 意识到；明白；知道
stay civil	to remain calm, or polite and cultured in a discussion 保持镇静，或者指在讨论中保持有礼貌和文明的
stay up	to go to bed later than usual 熬夜，深夜不睡

turn out that / to be	to be known or discovered finally and surprisingly 最终成为；最终发现
watch over somebody	to protect someone and make certain that he or she is safe 保护；照看
zoom in/out	to (cause a camera or computer to) make the image of something or someone appear much larger and nearer, or much smaller and further away（使照相机或计算机）画面放大 / 缩小

Task 1 Analytical Listening

Watch the video for the first time. Choose the best answer from the four choices marked A), B), C) and D).

1) When in college, Tim _____.
   A) got a job in government
   B) wrote a lot of papers
   C) was good at writing
   D) got "the best paper" award

2) Why does Tim want to write about procrastination?
   A) To prove he is amazing.
   B) To be a good writer.
   C) To explain to the non-procrastinators.
   D) To do a research.

3) The difference between procrastinators and non-procrastinators is that there is _____.
   A) a Rational Decision-Maker in the brain of a non-procrastinator
   B) a Rational Decision-Maker in the brain of a procrastinator
   C) an Instant Gratification Monkey in the brain of a non-procrastinator
   D) an Instant Gratification Monkey in the brain of a procrastinator

4) Which of the following statements is true about the Instant Gratification Monkey?
   A) It lives wholly in the present moment.
   B) It has memories about the past.
   C) It can predict the future.
   D) It cares about work and play.

5) Which of the following statements is **NOT** true about the Panic Monster?
   A) It always watches over the Instant Gratification Monkey.
   B) It suddenly wakes up anytime a deadline gets too close.
   C) It is the only thing the Instant Gratification Monkey is terrified of.
   D) It is awake most of the time.

6) According to Tim, the two types of procrastination are _____.
   A) fun things and easy things
   B) short-term goals and long-term goals
   C) situations with deadlines and without deadlines
   D) things that are visible and invisible

7) Tim mainly uses a Life Calendar to show _____.
   A) how long a life could be
   B) it is urgent to stay aware of procrastination
   C) what we procrastinate on
   D) everyone is procrastinating on something in life

8) This TED talk mainly discusses _____.
   A) the difference between the brains of a procrastinator and a non-procrastinator
   B) why procrastinators can do things more effectively
   C) different types of people who are procrastinating
   D) short-term and long-term procrastination

Task 2 Detailed Listening

Dictate the following sentences. All the sentences will be read four times.

1) _____

2) _____

3) _____

4) _____

5) _____

6) _____

7) _____

8) _____

Task 3 Critical Listening

Watch the video again and discuss the following questions with your language partner.

1) There are many "punch lines" that make this TED talk hilarious and inspiring. Please identify some and share your opinions about how they are organized at the linguistic level.

2) In the TED talk, Tim talks about pulling two all-nighters to write a paper which he was supposed to have spent a year on. Have you ever made a plan for homework but failed to follow it in a similar way? Do you think planning is useful for time management? Will the deadline of homework "kill" you or "save" you in terms of procrastination?

Speech Workshop

Retelling is an activity mostly used to promote comprehension as well as spoken vocabulary. During listening, you may note down both main ideas and supporting details as many as you can. Following your notes, it is suggested to retell what you hear in the order of "**topic sentence—supporting sentence—examples/details**". The following are two tips for you.

Tip 1: Use simple present tense or simple past tense to retell facts or others' stories in your own words. For example, Tim described his experience of procrastination in paper submission: "…pulling not one but two all-nighters—humans are not supposed to pull two all-nighters." You may retell it in this way: "Tim didn't like to remember the time when he pulled two all-nighters."

Tip 2: Use non-defining or defining relative clauses to combine more than one piece of information into one sentence. For example, Tim said, "I decided to write about procrastination. My behavior has always perplexed the non-procrastinators around me." You may retell the two sentences briefly as "Tim wanted to write about procrastination, which perplexes the non-procrastinators". In the Detailed Listening exercises of the TED talk "Inside the Mind of a Master Procrastinator", we have dictated sentences of both non-defining and defining relative clauses. Please read and compare:

Defining relative clause: *I had a hypothesis <u>that</u> the brains of procrastinators were actually different from the brains of other people.*

Non-defining relative clause: *In college, I was a government major, <u>which</u> meant I had to write a lot of papers.*

Task 1   Pair Work: Listen and Share

1) One student retells the talk "How to Study More Effectively" in terms of time-management tips. Please include both defining and non-defining relative clauses. After listening, another student reports orally about what is heard in an organized way.

2) One student retells the first part of the TED talk "Inside the Mind of a Master Procrastinator" in the order of "topic sentence–supporting sentence–examples/details". Please include both defining and non-defining relative clauses. After listening, another student reports orally about what is heard in an organized way.

Task 2   Unit Project

Research a typical working day of a student or a teacher in college. Please retell how he or she manages time in 1–2 minutes.

Pronunciation Workshop

Vowels

Knowing a language includes knowing the sounds of that language. The 26 English letters can be pronounced in at least 44 sounds, which are transcribed by phonetic symbols. The International Phonetic Alphabet (IPA) is devised to set a system in which there is a one-to-one correspondence between each sound in language and each phonetic symbol. For example, the word "procrastination" reads as /prəˌkræstɪ'neɪʃən/. The phonetic transcription is written between two backslash symbols (//) or square brackets ([ ]). In this transcription, there are five syllables. Each syllable consists of one or more letters with a **vowel** sound as its heart (Yoshida, 2016). A vowel is a speech sound where air leaves the mouth without any blockage by the tongue, lips, or throat. In English, vowels are represented by the letters "a", "e", "i", "o", "u", and sometimes "y".

Vowels are classified by how high or low the tongue is. The quality of a vowel is shown on a vowel quadrilateral (Figure 1.1) in terms of three basic variables (Reed & Levis, 2015): open/close; front/back; and rounded/unrounded. The first two depend on the position of the highest point of the tongue when producing the vowel. If the tongue is high in the mouth, we describe the vowel as close, while if it is low in the mouth, we say that the vowel is open; if the tongue is towards the front of the mouth, we describe the vowel as front, while if it is bunched at the back of the mouth, we say that it is a back vowel. The third variable depends on whether the lips are rounded or not. For example, the vowel in "food" (represented by the symbol /uː/ by most people in Britain, though many in North America prefer to show it as /u/) can be described as close back rounded, as the tongue is close to the roof and at the back of the mouth and the lips are rounded,

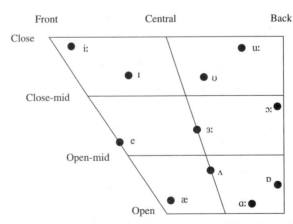

Figure 1.1　The monophthong vowels of British English

while /æ/, the vowel in "man", is open front unrounded, as the jaw is nearly fully open, the tongue is at the front of the mouth, and the lips are not rounded.

Apart from the **monophthongs** shown in Figure 1.1, a sequence of two vowel sounds pronounced together as one syllable is labeled as **diphthongs** such as /aɪ/ /eɪ/ /əʊ/ /aʊ/ /eə/ /ɪə/ /ɔɪ/ /ʊə/. To pronounce a diphthong, there is a noticeable sound change within the same syllable. The process of moving from one vowel sound to another gives a diphthong another name—gliding vowel. While vowel sounds do change in a diphthong, they do not necessarily take more time to pronounce than a monophthong.

There are more vowel contrasts in English than in Chinese, so English vowels are closer to each other in terms of position of articulation than Chinese vowels (Swan & Smith, 2001: 311). For example, the contrast between /iː/ and /ɪ/ has no equivalent in Chinese. The same applies to the contrast between /uː/ and /ʊ/. Therefore, students should practice differentiating words in pairs.

Task 1　Minimal Pairs

Listen and underline the word you hear.

1) back	buck	2) bean	bin	3) dive	Deve
4) ran	run	5) fool	full	6) Luke	look
7) shot	short	8) eat	it	9) cap	carp
10) at	ate	11) access	axis	12) mass	mice

Task 2　Tongue Twisters

Listen and read the tongue twisters with a focus on vowel sounds.

1) A flea and a fly were trapped in a flue, and they tried to flee for their life. The flea said to the fly "Let's flee!" and the fly said to the flea "Let's fly!" Finally both the flea and fly managed to flee through a flaw in the flue.

2) How much wood would a woodchuck chuck if a woodchuck could chuck wood? He would chuck, he would, as much as he could, and chuck as much wood as a woodchuck would if a woodchuck could chuck wood.

3) She sells seashells on the seashore. The shells she sells are seashells, I'm sure. And if she sells seashells on the seashore, then I'm sure she sells seashore shells.

Supplementary Materials

1. A conversation—"Time Management Tips"
2. A TED talk—"How to Gain Control of Your Free Time?"
3. A TED talk—"How to Manage Your Time More Effectively (According to Machines)?"
4. A lecture—"How to Schedule Your Day for Optimal Productivity?"
5. A TED talk—"3 Rules for Better Work-Life Balance"

Unit 2

Doing Research

1. *"We will fully implement the strategy for invigorating China through science and education, the workforce development strategy, and the innovation-driven development strategy."*

   —The Report to the 20th CPC National Congress

2. *"Great Learning aims to foster moral integrity, forge close ties with the people, and attain consummate virtue in both words and deeds."*

   —The Book of Rites

Lead-in

Lectures on academic topics often start with the phrase "research shows...". In fact, doing research is common and important for both teachers and students in college. It is also vitally important for carrying out the innovation-driven development strategy at the national level. Do you know what research is? How do you find research questions? What are the essential steps of conducting a research project? Please review the expressions from the Preparing to Speak box and use them in discussion with your classmates.

Preparing to Speak

Match the words and phrases with their definitions.

1. ethical principles
2. expertise
3. competence
4. data collection
5. interdisciplinary
6. methodology
7. observation
8. meta-analysis
9. assumption
10. criticism

a. collecting information about a particular subject
b. a system of ways of doing or studying something
c. a research method that combines results of related studies
d. codes of conduct about what is morally right and wrong
e. the art of evaluating or analyzing literature
f. a high level of knowledge or skill
g. something you accept as true without question or proof
h. the ability to do something well
i. the act of watching carefully in order to learn more
j. involving two or more different areas of knowledge

Learning Objectives

This unit will help you get the gist of the research steps as well as the research ethics. Upon completion of this unit, you will be able to

√ know the basic steps and ethical principles that govern doing research;

√ make a numbered list of main ideas and supporting details in the listening notes;

√ understand and apply consonant rules in pronunciation;

√ summarize what you hear concisely.

Unit 2
Doing Research

Listening Focus

Grouping Related Items

When you take notes while listening, **grouping related items** together will help you frame the main ideas and understand the relationship between different parts of the talk. There are different ways of organizing your notes, such as making a **numbered list** and sketching a **cluster web**.

A numbered list is a list of items or ideas indicated by numbers. While listening to a speech, one may list the specific number of ideas that are discussed. For example, a lecturer may say "There are three essential features of scientific research." or "Today we're going to focus on the six steps of writing a research report."

When you take notes, making a numbered list is important for understanding and remembering these points. Sometimes the speaker will refer back to earlier items, reviewing or adding new information to indicate the connection between those items. In this regard, you may note down the connection by using arrows. Here is an example of notes about the functions of a research project.

> A research project is used to:
> 1. establish or confirm facts;
> 2. reaffirm past work;
> 3. expand on past work;
> 4. solve new problems;
> 5. support theorems;
> 6. develop new theories.

Sometimes the speaker does not tell you the specific number of items, and you have to figure out the logical relationship between ideas during note-taking. It is helpful to note the cohesive devices used when introducing an item in a series, such as "in addition". Sketching a cluster web may also help you record complex information and visualize connections more easily. When you first listen to a speech, try to sketch a web out of the main ideas and then add more detailed information in the following listening. The following is an example of a cluster web about scientific empiricism. You should try to draw lines between the subtopics and their related details.

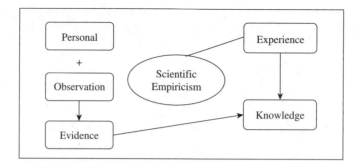

Listening Practice

Section A

Introduction to the listening material: This short video maps out the different steps to the scientific method, which was first acknowledged by Ibn al-Haytham. The speaker uses examples to illustrate the functions of this scientific procedure.

Glossary

Study the words and phrases in the glossary, especially the unfamiliar ones. Do you know how to pronounce or use them in sentences? Use a dictionary to find out more information if necessary.

Words

formulate	*v.*	to develop all the details of a plan for doing something 制订；规划；构想
genuine	*adj.*	real and exactly what something appears to be 真正的；非伪造的；名副其实的
optics	*n.*	the study of light and instruments using light 光学
phenomena	*n.*	(the plural form of phenomenon) things that exist and can be seen, felt, tasted, etc. 现象
reproducibility	*n.*	the fact that something is able to be shown, done, or made again 再现性；可重复性

solid	*adj.*	certain or safe; of a good standard; giving confidence or support 确定的；扎实的；可信赖的
variable	*n.*	a number, amount, or situation that can change 变量

Phrases

convert into	to (cause something or someone to) change in form or character（使）转变为……
rate the level of	to judge the value or character of someone or something 评价某人或某物的水平
vice versa	used to say that what you have just said is also true in the opposite order 反过来也一样，反之亦然
what if	used to ask about something that could happen in the future, especially something bad 如果……（尤指糟糕的情况出现）会怎么样？

Task 1   Analytical Listening

Watch the video and complete the outline of the talk.

The Scientific Method

Steps	Main Ideas
1	
2	
3	
4	
5	
6	

Task 2　Detailed Listening

Do the following statements agree with the information given in the talk? Watch the video again and decide whether they are

    T　(true) if the statement agrees with the information,

    F　(false) if the statement contradicts the information, or

    NG　(not given) if there is no information on this.

_____ 1) To find out the truth underlying curious phenomena in the world, we can follow a process known as the scientific method.

_____ 2) To come up with a question worth researching, we have to observe first.

_____ 3) After observation and formulation of a question, we should directly use a theory to test our prediction.

_____ 4) The example hypothesis—women smile more than men because they are happier than men—shows a point that we may borrow ideas from the literature review to formulate a hypothesis.

_____ 5) The complexity of hypothesis testing prevents us from finding the truth.

_____ 6) Once you have analyzed the data, you cannot change your hypothesis or the design of your testing.

_____ 7) The stage of analyzing and concluding can be repeated until you find the right hypothesis and test method to find accurate results.

_____ 8) In writing a research report or paper, we should not include incorrect predictions.

Task 3　Critical Listening

Watch the video for the third time and discuss the following questions with your language partner.

1) What should you do if you have discovered an even more interesting question (other than the current research question) after analyzing the data?

2) The speaker mentioned that "Reproducibility is a sign of good scientific work". Can you give any examples to illustrate this statement?

Section B

Introduction to the listening material: In this lecture—"Ethics in Research", the speaker discusses the meaning of ethics and its research application. This introduction to research ethics may help you become aware of what should or should not be done when undertake research.

Glossary

Study the words and phrases in the glossary, especially the unfamiliar ones. Do you know how to pronounce or use them in sentences? Use a dictionary to find out more information if necessary.

Words

autonomy	*n.*	the ability to make your own decisions without being controlled by anyone else 自主，自主权
confidentiality	*n.*	the state of being confidential 秘密性，机密性
consent	*n.*	permission or agreement 许可，允许；同意
consistency	*n.*	the quality of always behaving or performing in a similar way, or of always happening in a similar way 连贯性；一致性
constructive	*adj.*	If advice, criticism, or actions are constructive, they are useful and intended to help or improve something. 建设性的；有益的，有用的；积极的
dignity	*n.*	calm, serious, and controlled behavior that makes people respect you 庄重，端庄；尊严
dire	*adj.*	very serious or extreme 严重的；危急的；极端的
discrimination	*n.*	treating a person or particular group of people differently, especially in a worse way than the way in which you treat other people, because of their skin color, sex, sexuality, etc. 歧视；区别对待

disfigurement	*n.*	spoiling the appearance of something or someone, especially their face, completely 毁容
donor	*n.*	a person who gives money or goods to an organization 捐助者，捐赠者
duplicative	*adj.*	of, related to, or being a duplicate 复制的
ethnicity	*n.*	a particular race of people, or the fact of being from a particular race of people 族群
fabricate	*v.*	to invent or produce something false in order to deceive someone 捏造，虚构；伪造
fertilization	*n.*	the process of causing an egg or seed to start to develop into a new young animal or plant by joining it with a male cell 受精
indigenous	*adj.*	naturally existing in a place or country rather than arriving from another place 当地的；本土的，土生土长的
integrity	*n.*	the quality of being honest and having strong moral principles that you refuse to change 正直；诚实
legality	*n.*	the fact that something is allowed by the law 合法，合法性
malaria	*n.*	a disease that you can get from the bite of a particular type of mosquito (= a small flying insect) 疟疾
maturity	*n.*	a very advanced or developed form or state 成熟阶段；完善的状态
misconduct	*n.*	unacceptable or bad behavior by someone in a position of authority or responsibility 不端行为；失职；滥用职权
mitigate	*v.*	to make something less harmful, unpleasant, or bad 使缓和；减轻（危害等）
monitor	*v.*	to watch and check a situation carefully for a period of time in order to discover something about it 监控；监测；监视，密切注视
morality	*n.*	the quality of being right, honest, or acceptable 道德，道义
patent	*n.*	the official legal right to make or sell an invention for a particular number of years 专利权

plagiarism	*n.*	the process or practice of using another person's ideas or work and pretending that it is your own 剽窃，抄袭
precautionary	*adj.*	preventing something unpleasant or dangerous from happening 预防的；防备的
predatory	*adj.*	trying to get something that belongs to someone else（人或组织）掠夺（性）的，掠夺成性的
regime	*n.*	a particular government or a system or method of government 政府；政权；政体
rigor	*n.*	the quality of being detailed, careful, and complete 严密；缜密；严谨
sterilization	*n.*	the process of having a medical operation to make it impossible to have children 绝育，结扎
transplantation	*n.*	the act of moving something from one place to another 转移
trauma	*n.*	a severe emotional shock and pain caused by an extremely upsetting experience 精神创伤，心理创伤
volunteer	*v.*	to offer to do something that you do not have to, often without having been asked to do it and/or without expecting payment 自愿做；无偿做；做志愿者；主动提出做

Phrases

and the like	(informal) and similar things 等等，之类
aside from	except for 除……以外
be concerned with	to be about a particular thing or person 涉及某事或某人
concentration camp	a place where large numbers of people are kept as prisoners in extremely bad conditions, especially for political reasons 集中营
intellectual property	someone's idea, invention, creation, etc., that can be protected by law from being copied by someone else 知识产权

needless to say	as you would expect; added to, or used to introduce, a remark giving information that is expected and not surprising 当然，不用说
peer review	the process of someone reading, checking, and giving his or her opinion about something that has been written by another scientist or expert working in the same subject area, or a piece of work in which this is done（学术出版过程中的）同行审议
strive to/for	to try very hard to do something or to make something happen, especially for a long time or against difficulties（尤指长期或不畏艰难地）努力，奋斗，力争

Task 1 Analytical Listening

Watch the video for the first time, cluster related ideas, and complete the outline of the talk.

Ethics in Research

Subtopics	Clustering Related Ideas
The definition of ethics	Ethics is the (1) _____ of a human act.
The importance of ethics	– Ethics matters because it (2) _____ to others and (3) _____ of what we do. – As a branch of philosophy, ethics provides rules that (4) _____. – Ethics allows researchers and scholars to further (5) _____ themselves and (6) _____ their activities.
Researchers' obligations	– Moral obligation: (7) _____ to the participants. – Research misconduct: e.g., Nazi human (8) _____ Nazi medical doctors forced (9) _____ prisoners to participate in the experiment. No consent was given for the (10) _____.

(Continued)

Subtopics	Clustering Related Ideas
Ethical principles	– Honesty—Researchers should not falsify, (11) _____, and misrepresent data and results.
	– Objectivity—Researchers should strive to avoid all forms of (12) _____ in research.
	– (13) _____—Protect confidential communications.
	– Competence—Be competent scholars.
	– Integrity—Strive for (14) _____ in thought and action.
	– (15) _____—Obey laws and policies.
	– Maturity and openness—Be open to (16) _____ and new ideas.
	– Respect for (17) _____.
	– Responsible publication—Avoid (18) _____ publication.
	– Non-discrimination
	– Human subjects protection—Respect human dignity, privacy, and (19) _____ at all times.
	– Animal care
	– Social responsibility—Strive to promote social good and (20) _____

Task 2 Detailed Listening

Listen to the ethical principles and then decide whether the following statements are

      T (true) if the statement agrees with the information,

      F (false) if the statement contradicts the information, or

      NG (not given) if there is no information on this.

_____ 1) The peer review process and grant writing are not free from bias.

_____ 2) Papers or grants submitted for publications and patient records are examples of confidential communications in research.

_____ 3) Improving professional competence and expertise is one of the obligations of researchers.

_____ 4) Honesty and integrity in research ethics are the same.

_____ 5) Because of confidentiality, researchers should not share data and resources.

_____ 6) Under no circumstances should researchers use methods, data, and results owned by other researchers or scholars.

_____ 7) Senior researchers have to promote the welfare of their students and allow them to make their own decisions.

_____ 8) Respecting animal rights means that researchers should not use animals in research.

Task 3　Critical Listening

Watch the video again and discuss the following questions with your language partner.

1) Ethical principles state that researchers should avoid plagiarism at all times. In the era of artificial intelligence, especially with the rise of ChatGPT, how should we define and avoid plagiarism?

2) Researchers need to publish books or papers in order to advance knowledge and scholarships and not merely their own careers. How do you understand the saying "publish or perish" in terms of the ethical principles regarding responsible publication?

Speech Workshop

Oral summary has been proven to be effective in vocabulary learning among intermediate-level English learners (Tabrizi & Abbasi, 2016). It is also a fluency activity to process the information you hear. Different from retelling or recounting, however, summarizing requires a focus on the main points of the listening material and their logical connections. While listening, you should cluster the evidence that the speaker uses to support the main points. Here are some useful tips for summarizing what you hear (Seyler, 2013: 10–11).

Tip 1: To signal, it is suggested to begin with a reference to the speaker or title of what you hear, and then state the thesis. For example, if you summarize your group discussion, you may start with "Our group discussed three main aspects of research, namely, what research is, why we should conduct research, and how we do it". In the above statement, "Our group" is a reference to the speaker, and the "three main aspects..." is the thesis of the oral summary. You should then briefly summarize each of the three aspects.

Tip 2: Do not include your personal reflections or misrepresent the original idea. Summary is an objective and abstract restatement of the main ideas. You should combine the main ideas into fewer sentences than were used in the original. For example, in a group discussion, students may give many examples. When you summarize your group discussion, examples should be categorized to illustrate the main points without presenting details.

Tip 3: Keep the parts of your summary in the same proportions as in the original. For example, if the speaker devotes about 20 percent of words on the first point of the speech, then that idea should get about 20 percent of the length of time in your oral summary.

Task 1 Pair Work: Listen and Share

1) Both students in each pair contribute an example of research. Listen to each other and take notes.

2) Based on those examples, discuss the essential aspects of research, i.e., what research is.

3) Condense your ideas into an oral summary. Share it with your classmates.

Task 2 Unit Project

Your class is going to hold an English panel discussion on research ethics. Form a group of 3–5 students. Your group is suggested to conduct a mini-research on campus to investigate students' perceptions of plagiarism. You should then summarize your major findings to make an oral group report. Both primary and secondary resources can be used in your oral summary.

Pronunciation Workshop

Consonants

Vowels do not touch the mouth at all during speech, while consonants do at some point. Consonants can be grouped by the **place of articulation**. For example, some consonants are articulated with the lips such as /p/, /b/, /m/, /f/, /v/, /w/, and some are articulated by raising the blade of the tongue, such as /θ/, /ð/, /t/, /d/, /n/, /s/, /z/, /ʃ/, /ʒ/, /tʃ/, /dʒ/, /l/, and /r/. Recognizing the place of articulation is helpful to understand connected speech or liaison (see Pronunciation Workshop in Unit 3).

Consonants can also be classified according to whether they are **voiced** or **voiceless**. If you put your fingers on your throat and utter /b/, you should feel a vibration from your throat in your fingers. Whereas, if you say /t/, you will feel that your fingers don't vibrate. Therefore, /b/ is a voiced consonant sound while /t/ is voiceless.

However, the **manner of articulation**, which is concerned with the airflow, is more important for you to grasp the essence of consonant production. Table 2.1 maps out the different ways in which the airstream is used to produce different consonant sounds.

Table 2.1 The manner of articulation for English consonants

Manner of Articulation	Definition	Examples
Plosive	stop the flow of air at some point and suddenly release it	/p/ /t/ /k/ /b/ /d/ /g/
Fricative	squeeze air through a small hole or gap in your mouth	/f/ /v/ /θ/ /ð/ /s/ /z/ /ʃ/ /ʒ/
Affricate	stop immediately followed by a fricative	/tʃ/ /dʒ/
Nasal	velum lowered and air goes through the nasal cavity	/m/ /n/ /ŋ/
Liquid	the air is blocked but escapes through the sides	/l/ /r/
Approximant	the airflow is impeded only slightly	/w/ /j/ /r/

Some consonant sounds are not easy for Chinese learners because they are absent from Chinese dialects (Swan & Smith, 2001). For example, /v/ is absent from most

Chinese dialects and therefore it is sometimes treated like /w/ or /f/: "invite" may be mispronounced /ɪnwaɪt/; "live" may be mispronounced /lif/. Final consonants also cause a problem as you tend either to add an extra vowel at the end, or to drop the consonant and produce a slight glottal or unreleased stop. Therefore, you are suggested to follow the recordings of listening practice and correct pronunciation accordingly.

Task 1   Minimal Pairs

Listen and underline the word you hear.

1) lock   rock   2) need   lead   3) snack   slack

4) vine   wine   5) verse   worse   6) leaf   leave

7) both   boat   8) fool   pool   9) west   vest

10) sin   thin   11) tickets ticket   12) zeal   seal

Task 2   Tongue Twisters

Listen and read the tongue twisters with a focus on consonant sounds.

1) Peter Piper picked a peck of pickled peppers.

   Did Peter Piper pick a peck of pickled peppers?

   If Peter Piper picked a peck of pickled peppers,

   Where's the peck of pickled peppers Peter Piper picked?

2) Fuzzy Wuzzy was a bear,

   Fuzzy Wuzzy had no hair,

   Fuzzy Wuzzy wasn't really fuzzy, was he?

Supplementary Materials

1. A lecture—"What Is Research?"

2. A TED talk—"Why You Should Love Statistics?"

3. A lecture—"Describing Statistics"

4. A lecture—"Avoiding Plagiarism"

5. A lecture—"How to Develop a Good Research Topic?"

Unit 3

Happiness

1. *"Success is not the key to happiness. Happiness is the key to success. If you love what you are doing, you will be successful."*

   —Albert Schweitzer (1875–1965), German musician, philosopher, theologian, and Nobel Prize-winning physician

2. *"The supreme happiness of life is the conviction that we are loved."*

   —Victor Hugo (1802–1885), French novelist, poet, and dramatist of the Romantic Movement

Lead-in

Both Confucius and Socrates said that happiness is the purpose of life. Everyone chases the feeling of being happy. But what is the meaning of "happiness"? What makes people happy? Interview students in your group about what makes them happy and summarize the answers. Please review the expressions from the Preparing to Speak box and use them in discussion with your classmates.

Preparing to Speak

Match the words and phrases with their definitions.

1. individual
2. self-fulfillment
3. hedonism
4. philosophy
5. self-worth
6. fame
7. glamorous
8. go after
9. tend to
10. optimism

a. the way that someone thinks about life and deals with it
b. the value you give to your life and achievements
c. attractive in an exciting and special way
d. a single person or thing
e. to deal with the problems or needs of a person or thing
f. a feeling of satisfaction when you achieve what is wanted
g. the quality of being full of hope
h. the belief that the most important thing in life is to enjoy
i. to chase or follow someone or something
j. the state of being well known because of achievements

Learning Objectives

This unit will lead you to ponder over the sources of real happiness from a psychological perspective. Upon completion of this unit, you will be able to

√ describe and interpret psychological well-being;

√ activate relevant background knowledge to understand the implied meaning of words and expressions;

√ identify and apply liaison in pronunciation;

√ review others' speeches with reasonable insight.

Listening Focus

Implied Meaning

Implied meaning refers to the meaning behind one's words or the meaning between the lines. In listening practices, typical questions concerning implied meaning are:

- What can be inferred about X?
- What does ××× imply about X?
- What will ××× probably do next?
- What does ××× imply/mean when he or she says this?

For example, two students go into a classroom, and one female student says, "Gosh, it's freezing! Peter, you're near the window. Would you mind?"

What does the student imply when she says this?

(A) Asking a favor of Peter. (B) Complaining about something Peter has done.

The **literal meaning**, which refers to information given directly, is a statement of fact and inquiry. However, in real communication, the information is not always given straightforwardly. When meaning is implied, you should make connections between the literal information and the relevant background knowledge. In the above example, you may draw on common sense or activate your relevant knowledge to infer the implied meaning, which is to ask a favor of Peter rather than complain about something Peter has done. Therefore, inferring the meaning of utterances or cultural connotations based on the context is critical to listening comprehension.

The **implied meaning** is determined through understanding the context of the passage surrounding the sentence in question. Therefore, **considering the context** is key when trying to understand the implied meaning of a speaker's words. Context mainly refers to the situation, the relationship between the speaker and the listener, and the overall atmosphere of the conversation. Relevant general knowledge will also help you make connections. All of these can provide clues as to what the speaker is really trying to say. Besides, listening for patterns also helps you understand the implied meaning of the speaker's words, which involves looking for particular words or phrases that the speaker uses repeatedly.

Listening Practice

Section A

Introduction to the listening material: In this interview, David Moser, a sinologist and linguist who began his research on China in the 1980s, tells CGTN anchor Tian Wei that the notion of happiness is not really a matter of sensual pleasure, but something of a collective phenomenon for Confucius. He believes the Confucian concept of happiness can inspire today's conflicted Western society.

Glossary

Study the words and phrases in the glossary, especially the unfamiliar ones. Do you know how to pronounce or use them in sentences? Use a dictionary to find out more information if necessary.

Words

augment	v.	to increase the size or value of something by adding something to it 提高；增大；加强
collaboration	n.	the situation of two or more people working together to create or achieve the same thing 合作；协作
collective	adj.	of or shared by every member of a group of people 集体的；共同的
collectivism	n.	a theory or political system based on the principle that all of the farms, factories, and other places of work in a country should be owned by or for all the people in that country 集体主义；集体主义制度
compromise	n.	an agreement in an argument in which the people involved reduce their demands or change their opinion in order to agree 妥协；折中；让步；和解
Confucian	adj.	based on or believing in the ideas of the Chinese philosopher Confucius 孔子的；儒家的，儒学的，儒教的

Confucianism	*n.*		a religion based on the ideas of the Chinese philosopher Confucius 孔子学说；儒学，儒教
Confucius	*n.*		a Chinese philosopher, politician, and teacher, who lived from 551 BCE–479 BCE 孔子（公元前 551—前 479 年，中国哲学家、政治家和教育家）
convey	*v.*		to express a thought, feeling, or idea so that it is understood by other people 表达，传达（思想、感情或想法）
cross-cultural	*adj.*		involving two or more different cultures and their ideas and customs 跨文化的
dopamine	*n.*		a hormone (= chemical substance) that is made naturally in the body and may also be given as a drug 多巴胺
flourish	*v.*		to grow or develop successfully 茁壮成长；繁荣；蓬勃发展
gesture	*n.*		a movement of the hands, arms, or head, etc. to express an idea or feeling 手势；姿势；示意动作
holistic	*adj.*		dealing with or treating the whole of something or someone and not just a part 整体的，全面的
individualism	*n.*		the idea that freedom of thought and action for each person is the most important quality of a society, rather than shared effort and responsibility 个人主义
negotiation	*n.*		the process of discussing something with someone in order to reach an agreement with them, or the discussions themselves 谈判，磋商，洽谈
opposing	*adj.*		competing or fighting against each other 对立的，对抗的
optimal	*adj.*		best; most likely to bring success or advantage 最优的，最佳的；优化的
paramount	*adj.*		more important than anything else 至上的，首要的
ritual	*n.*		a set of fixed actions and sometimes words performed regularly, especially as part of a ceremony 例行公事，老规矩；（尤指）仪式
salute	*v.*		(especially of people in the armed forces) to make a formal sign of respect to someone, especially by raising the right hand to the side of the head（尤指军人）敬礼

schism	n.	a division into two groups caused by a disagreement about ideas, especially in a religious organization（尤指教会的）分裂
sensual	adj.	expressing or suggesting physical, especially sexual, pleasure or satisfaction 感官的；（尤指）肉欲的，愉悦肉体的，满足肉欲的
subservience	n.	a willingness to do what other people want, or the act of considering your wishes as less important than those of other people 恭顺，屈从；低声下气
superior	n.	a person or group of people who are higher in rank or social position than others 上司，上级
unamenable	adj.	not willing to accept or be influenced by a suggestion 不可修复的；不承担责任的

Phrases

and so forth	together with other similar things 等等
be accompanied by	to go with someone or to be provided or exist at the same time as something 陪同，陪伴；伴随，和……一起发生（或存在）
by contrast	when examined together with another person or thing to find the differences between them 对照，对比
capital punishment	punishment by death, as ordered by a legal system 死刑，极刑
have a handle on	to understand and be able to deal with (something) 理解并能够处理（某事物）
in conjunction with	when events or conditions combine or happen together 结合；联合；同时发生
reach (a) consensus	to come to an agreement 达成一致的意见；达成共识
spell...out	to explain something in a very clear way with details 解释清楚；详细地说明

Unit 3 Happiness

Task 1 Analytical Listening

Watch the video for the first time and complete the outline of the interview.

Confucian Philosophy on Happiness

Stages of the Interview	Answers from the Interviewee
Defining happiness in terms of the Confucian concept	– Different from the West, Confucian philosophy sees happiness as a sort of (1) _____. – Confucian notion of a good life: Happiness is not a matter of (2) _____, but more of a(n) (3) _____. – Western societies see the unit of culture as (4) _____. Confucius saw the basic unit of society as (5) _____.
The influences of the Confucian concept in the West	– Confucianism is getting popular in the West and the hardest aspect for students is the notion of (6) _____. It helps the West develop a better system of explaining (7) _____. – One of the biggest influences of Confucianism now in the West is (8) _____. – The way to solve the conflict in the West in terms of moral philosophy: Setting the tone of (9) _____.

Task 2 Detailed Listening

Match the details with their implied meaning.

Details	Implied Meaning
1) There are a lot of words related to happiness: Desire, pleasure, hedonism, and so on. So to Confucius, it's none of those words alone.	a. Lack of ritual may lead to unhappy feelings.
2) The feeling of what a good life would be, is not one of self-fulfillment, but of the total fulfillment of all those connections in your life.	b. Everything in life including nonverbal messages can be meaningful to communicate or interact with others.

39

3) The way you use your body in everyday life and the way you use your face and your head convey the different kinds of connectiveness that we have.

4) One of the reasons we're so unhappy now is that we're doing all these interactions online, where you can't see the ritual gestures, the pat on the back, the hug…

5) We (Western people) tend to see people as maximizing the happiness of the individual and all the other things will fall into place or finding out that is absolutely not the case.

c. The notion of happiness is not a kind of physical, sensual pleasure.

d. Maximizing the happiness of the individual cannot offer a good solution to all problems.

e. Happiness is not confined to an individual but more about the well-being of a family or a society.

Task 3 Critical Listening

Watch the video again and discuss the following questions with your language partner.

1) According to Hofstede's cultural dimension theory, the individualism-collectivism dimension relates to a societal, not an individual's, characteristic and identifies the extent to which people in a society are integrated into groups. How does this cultural dimension affect the pursuit of happiness in different cultural groups?

2) The speaker mentions that one of the most popular courses at Harvard University is a course on Chinese philosophy. Why has Chinese philosophy such as Confucianism gained popularity in the West?

Introduction to the listening material: In this TED talk—"What Makes a Good Life? Lessons from the Longest Study on Happiness", Robert Waldinger has presented research findings on true happiness. As the director of a 75-year-old study on adult development, Robert shares three important lessons learned from the study.

Unit 3 Happiness

Glossary

Study the words and phrases in the glossary, especially the unfamiliar ones. Do you know how to pronounce or use them in sentences? Use a dictionary to find out more information if necessary.

Words

alcoholism	*n.*	the condition of being an alcoholic 酗酒
bickering	*n.*	arguments about things that are not important 斗嘴，口角
cholesterol	*n.*	a substance containing a lot of fat that is found in the body tissue and blood of all animals, thought to be part of the cause of heart disease if there is too much of it 胆固醇
committed	*adj.*	loyal and willing to give your time and energy to something that you believe in 忠诚的；坚定的；尽职尽责的
constantly	*adv.*	all the time or often 总是；经常地，不断地
dedicated	*adj.*	believing that something is very important and giving a lot of time and energy to it 尽心尽力的，尽职尽责的
divorce	*v.*	to end your marriage by an official or legal process （与……）离婚
downright	*adj.*	(especially of something bad) extremely or very great（尤指不好的事情）极端的，极大的，十足的
exceedingly	*adv.*	to a very great degree 非常；特别；极其
feud	*n.*	an argument that has existed for a long time between two people or groups, causing a lot of anger or violence 宿怨；世仇；长期争斗
funding	*n.*	money given by a government or organization for an event or activity 资助，资金提供
grudge	*n.*	a strong feeling of anger and dislike for a person who you feel has treated you badly, especially one that lasts for a long time 怨恨，嫌隙，积怨

hindsight	n.	the ability to understand an event or situation only after it has happened 事后聪明，事后的认识
isolated	adj.	feeling unhappy because of not seeing or talking to other people 被孤立的，孤独的
magnify	v.	to make something look larger than it is, especially by looking at it through a lens 放大，扩大
millennial	n.	(usually plural) a person born in the 1980s or 1990s 千禧世代
octogenarian	n.	a person who is between 80 and 89 years old 八旬老人，80至89岁的人
period	n.	the symbol used in writing at the end of a sentence or the end of the short form of a word 句号
persistence	n.	the fact that someone or something persists 持续存在；坚持不懈，执意
questionnaire	n.	a list of questions that several people are asked so that information can be collected about something 问卷；情况调查表
schizophrenia	n.	a serious mental illness in which someone cannot understand what is real and what is imaginary 精神分裂症
sling	n.	a simple weapon used mainly in the past in which a strap held at the ends was used for throwing stones（旧时用作武器的）投石器，弹弓
sophomore	n.	a student studying in the second year of a course at a U.S. college or high school (= a school for students aged 15 to 18)（美国大学或高中的）二年级学生
stale	adj.	used to describe someone who has lost interest in what he or she is doing because of being bored or working too hard（对所做之事）厌倦的，腻烦的
survive	v.	to continue to live or exist, especially after coming close to dying or being destroyed or after being in a difficult or threatening situation 继续生存，存活；（尤指）幸存
tenement	n.	a large building divided into apartments, usually in a poor area of a city（常指城市贫民区的）公寓大楼

toxic	*adj.*	causing you a lot of harm and unhappiness over a long period of time 恶毒的；造成阴影的
track	*v.*	to follow a person or animal by looking for proof that they have been somewhere, or by using electronic equipment 跟踪，追踪
unfold	*v.*	If a situation or story unfolds, it develops or becomes clear to other people.（形势或故事）发展，展现，呈现，披露
vast	*adj.*	extremely big 巨大的；广大的

Phrases

all walks of life	different types of jobs and different levels of society 各行各业；各个社会阶层
bicker with somebody	to argue with somebody about things that are not important （为小事）争吵，发生口角，斗嘴
buffer from	to provide protection against harm 提供保护，使不受伤害
count on somebody	to be confident that you can depend on someone 依靠……；指望……
day in (and) day out	(especially of something boring) done or happening every day for a long period of time（尤指枯燥之事）一天接一天，日复一日
drop out of	to not do something that you were going to do, or to stop doing something before you have completely finished 停止；退出；中断
fall apart	to fail or stop working effectively 破裂；解体，瓦解
go through	to continue firmly or obstinately to the end 经历；经受
in the midst of	in the middle of an event, a situation, or an activity 正当……的时候；在……之中
in one's 90s	between the ages of 90 and 99 九十多岁
lean in (to)	to pursue some task or activity with great effort, determination, and perseverance 全力以赴完成某项任务、活动等

liven... up	to become more energetic or in a better mood, or to make someone feel this way（使）（某人）振作起来；（使）（某人）快乐起来
quick fix	something that seems to be a fast and easy solution to a problem but is in fact not very good or will not last long（不完善的）应急解决办法，权宜之计
running water	water supplied to a house by pipes 自来水
take a toll on	to cause suffering, deaths, or damage 造成损失（或伤亡、破坏）

Task 1 Analytical Listening

Watch the video for the first time and complete the outline of the talk.

What Makes a Good Life?
Lessons from the Longest Study on Happiness

Introduction to the study	**The Harvard Study of Adult Development** Since the year (1) _____, we've tracked the lives of (2) _____—from teenagers to (3) _____.
Three important lessons learned from the study	The clearest message that we get from this study is that: (4) _____ keep us happier and healthier. – **Lesson 1** (5) _____ are really good for us, and (6) _____ kills. – **Lesson 2** It's not just the number of friends you have, but it's the (7) _____ that matters. – **Lesson 3** Good relationships don't just protect our bodies, they protect our (8) _____.
Conclusion	The good life is built with (9) _____.

Task 2 Detailed Listening

Watch the video clips and answer the following questions briefly.

1) At the beginning of the talk, the speaker claims that "Hindsight is anything but 20/20". What can be implied from this sentence?

2) Listen to a segment of this talk and specify the meaning of each of the following figures. For example, 75 is specified as *75 years of the study*.

   a. 724 _____

   b. 60 _____

   c. 90s _____

   d. 2000 _____

3) Listen to a segment of this talk and describe the two groups of men in the study.

4) When the inner Boston men ask about why the researchers keep studying them, what do they probably mean? What does the speaker imply when he says "The Harvard men never ask that question"?

5) When the research team asked the wives of the participants if they would join as members of the study, the wives said, "You know, it's about time." What can be inferred from this response?

Task 3 Critical Listening

Watch the video again and discuss the following questions with your language partner.

1) The longest study on happiness has revealed that good relationships are the key. To what extent do you agree that the experience of loneliness makes people less happy?

2) In the TED talk, the speaker presents some research details, such as the methods, participants, and findings. From the perspective of doing research, are there any ethical issues involved in this study? What do you suggest improving this study in the following years?

Speech Workshop

Reviewing

Oral reviewing can be an effective learning technique to practice speech fluency and cultivate critical thinking. Giving pertinent reviews or comments on other people's speeches is also one of the basic skills for academic English. When you orally review others' points of view, you have to retell or summarize others' words briefly and then evaluate the ideas as well as the information they have presented. In a word, through reviewing you will examine others' thoughts on a topic from your point of view. The following are some tips for you.

Tip 1: Try to start your review with a summary of the speech. For example, if you review the TED talk "What Makes a Good Life? Lessons from the Longest Study on Happiness", you may start with a statement like "The key message from this talk is…" or "What I learned from this speech is…". Summarizing the key message from the talk under review will make sure that you have listened carefully and comprehensively in order not to misunderstand others.

Tip 2: Pick a perspective to review based on your audience. You can review basically anything in a speech such as the content, organization, and style. But the best way to present your opinion depends on who your audience is. If you are in a class debate, for example, it is better to first clearly state what your main objection to the argument is, and then offer your own reasons to support your disagreement. To organize your review, you may consider the following questions to pick a perspective.

- Was the content clear and well-articulated?
- Was the argument supported with research or good examples?
- Was the content made clear to the audience?
- Did the speaker prove his or her points?
- Was the supporting argument logically structured?
- Was the speech easy to follow? Why?
- Did the speaker's points flow logically from one to the next?
- How would you describe the style of the speech and the speaker?

Tip 3: Try to find at least one positive point to include. A critical review may start with a compliment on an aspect of the talk in goodwill. The review would be more credible if it admits both the positive and the negative parts. It is important to make all feedback constructive, not destructive.

Tip 4: Personalize your oral review. You may relate the review directly to your personal experience. It strengthens the credibility of your review when you cannot find other reliable sources to support a point. Personal experience may also help hook the audience and draw them in.

Tip 5: Use hedges to invite alternative viewpoints. **Hedges** (Hyland, 2005) are expressions such as "possible", "might", and "plausibly", which emphasize the subjectivity of a position by allowing information to be presented as an opinion rather than a fact and therefore open that position to negotiation. Useful hedges in an oral review are but not limited to the following examples:

- The chances are (good) that…
- It could be the case that…
- It is likely to result in…
- It might be suggested that…
- It appears to suggest that…
- One possible implication of this is that…
- The evidence from this research indicates that…

Task 1   Pair Work: Listen and Share

1) Organize a pair discussion on the topic of happiness. One student starts by reviewing the TED talk—"What Makes a Good Life? Lessons from the Longest Study on Happiness".

2) Another student takes notes to comment on the other student's words.

Task 2   Unit Project

Happiness is different in people's eyes. For example, the Danish secret to achieving happiness is labeled as *hygge*, which comes from doing simple things such as lighting candles, baking, or spending time at home with family. Research the definition of happiness from a cross-cultural perspective by interviewing people from different cultures. And then report your findings in class.

Pronunciation Workshop

Liaison

In a natural speech, words are not pronounced one by one. Usually, the end of one word attaches to the beginning of the next word. This is called **liaison** in pronunciation, also known as **connected speech or linking**, a way of joining the pronunciation of two words so that they are easy to speak and flow together smoothly. Words are connected in four main situations, as shown in Table 3.1.

Table 3.1　Rules of connected speech in English

Liaison Rules	Definitions
Consonant to vowel	A word ending with a consonant sound is linked to a word beginning with a vowel sound. The consonant seems to become part of the following word.
Identical consonant	Words are connected when a word ends in a consonant sound and the next one starts with a consonant that is in a similar position (the lips, behind the teeth, or in the throat).
Vowel to vowel	When a word ending in a vowel sound is next to one beginning with a vowel sound, they are connected with a glide between the two vowels. A glide is either a slight /j/ sound or a slight /w/ sound.
t, d, s, or z + y	When the letter or sound of t, d, s, or z is followed by a word that starts with y, or its sound, both sounds are connected.

Task 1　Sample Analysis

Listen to the following roundtable discussion on happiness provided by Tina Yun, an English lecturer at Tsinghua University. Identify different types of liaison (underlined).

Moderator: Okay, so today we_are going to have_our roundtable discussion. I know you have_all prepared well for this. Our guiding question for today_is what makes_someone happy. Before we begin, let's cover some expectations and ground rules. We will start with Oliver and then move on to Sophie on his left and continue in this clockwise direction. You may refer to your notes but be sure not to stare at your notes. Each speaker will have up to 2 minutes to present their ideas. Once everyone has shared, the floor will be opened for any questions or comments you may have for each other. Please try to come up with at least one question or comment for each speaker. Oliver, are you ready?

Oliver: Sure. I think that staying healthy through getting enough exercise and eating right are key to making someone happy. As the saying goes, health is everything. Without health, you are nothing. That's why oftentimes when people want to revamp their lives, they start with waking up early and working out. The idea is that once you acquire one good habit, other good habits follow. In fact, I'm listening to an audiobook right now called *The Power of Habit* and that's what the author said.

Moderator: Alright. Sophie?

Sophie: From my personal experience and others I have talked to for this discussion, I firmly believe that relationships with close ones and the community play the largest roles in whether someone is happy. Life is meaningless without people to share my experiences with. The support I've received from my friends has gotten me through my darkest days. I've also learned over the years to not make needless comparisons with others but to share in the joy of those close to me. After graduation, I would love to go back to my hometown and give back to the community that has given so much to me.

Task 2 Listen and Identify: Liaison

Listen to the rest part of this roundtable discussion on happiness. Underline the liaison and practice reading it.

Moderator: Thanks for sharing. Luke?

Luke: I have two points. The first is that everyone needs to be grateful to enjoy happiness. The issue is that happiness is right in front of many people, but they don't realize it because they always want more. The second point is that people need a purpose or a goal they are working towards. When this has been found, work no longer feels like work and is pleasurable instead.

Moderator: Alright. Thank you all. A number of points were brought up. Would anyone like to make any comments?

Sophie: Oliver, I do think that having good health makes life more convenient and perhaps productive. However, I disagree that health is "everything" and that you are nothing without health. For example, I have diabetes. Closely monitoring my diet and getting more exercise to keep my blood sugar under control seemed like a burden at first. However, when you put diabetes aside, I've gotten healthier overall. Getting diabetes motivated me to take better care of myself. Furthermore, I developed compassion for people with other health issues. So I think I'm actually a better person now, with "more" to who I am, so to speak.

Oliver: I didn't think of it that way before. Glad you brought that up!

Moderator: Yes, what a great example! Anyone else have something?

Luke: Before I start, I want to say that I totally agree with Sophie that relationships bring us a lot of support. The saying goes that good friends are hard to find and even harder to keep. While friends are important, I believe that friends come and go. Besides, bad friends take away a lot of our time and energy. If you believe in the wrong person, the time and energy spent on them can't be given back. It might be best to just focus on your own personal goals. At least you can always trust and rely on yourself.

Sophie: Well, of course there's always some risk when you don't know someone well. But in a friendship, you don't just give. You also take when the need arises. It doesn't matter that our paths may divide because sharing happy moments in the present matters most.

Moderator: Let me just step in here. Luke and Sophie value different things in friendship, and they're all valid points. This leads us to question whether there is one single definition of happiness that applies to everyone. Oliver?

Oliver: Probably not. Two people can have the same experience but react to it very differently. While people share commonalities, individuals may have different ideas of happiness depending on their personalities and experiences.

Moderator: Very well. And I just realized that our time is almost up for today. Sorry, we didn't get to discuss your thoughts, Luke. We had a lively discussion about the effects of exercise, relationships, gratitude, and goals on happiness. Furthermore, it was noted that individuals vary in their perception of happiness depending on who they are and their experiences. Any last comments before we go? OK, I guess not. Thank you, everyone.

Supplementary Materials

1. A BBC talk—"Workplace Happiness"

2. A TED talk—"A Simple Strategy for Happiness"

3. A CGTN interview—"The Danish Secret to Achieving Happiness"

Unit 4

Depression

1. "All stress, anxiety, depression, is caused when we ignore who we are, and start living to please others."

—Paulo Coelho (1947–), Brazilian lyricist and novelist

2. "You are valuable just because you exist. Not because of what you do or what you have done, but simply because you are."

—Max Lucado (1955–), American author and minister at Oak Hills Church in San Antonio, Texas

Lead-in

Mental health issues such as depression and anxiety can have a major impact on people's quality of life, affecting everything from their relationships to their ability to work or study. These conditions are increasingly common, particularly among young people. What is mental health in your mind? How do you assess your own mental health? What can you do to help people suffering from mental illness? Please review the expressions from the Preparing to Speak box and use them in discussion with your classmates.

Preparing to Speak

Match the words and phrases with their definitions.

1. vary
2. clinical
3. concentrate
4. depression
5. gene
6. mood disorder
7. motivate
8. negative
9. symptom
10. up to

a. a mental health disorder characterized by persistent feelings of sadness and hopelessness
b. a physical or mental condition that is indicative of a disease
c. a piece of DNA molecule that determines a hereditary characteristic
d. a mental health condition characterized by severe or frequent changes in mood
e. indicating the limit of something, or the highest amount or level that can be reached
f. to change or be different according to the situation
g. to focus one's attention or effort on a particular task or activity
h. relating to the diagnosis and treatment of medical or mental health conditions by professionals
i. to drive someone to take action, typically to achieve a goal or desired outcome
j. having an unfavorable or unhelpful effect or impact

Learning Objectives

This unit will guide you to understand the causes, symptoms, and treatments of depression. Upon completion of this unit, you will be able to

√ understand mental health comprehensively;

Unit 4
Depression

- √ know how to use details to illustrate concepts or support ideas;
- √ apply loss of plosion in pronunciation;
- √ analyze and develop an informative speech.

Listening Focus

Details

In listening, **details** play an important role in comprehension. **Specific words and nonverbal cues** are essential for understanding the meaning, tone, and intention behind the speaker's message. This will enable listeners to interpret the spoken content more accurately.

Additionally, focusing on details can enhance vocabulary acquisition, and improve pronunciation and speaking skills. Noticing specifics in conversations facilitates learning new words and phrases. Meanwhile, listening to subtle differences in intonation, stress, and rhythm aids in accurately replicating the sounds of the target language, thus improving speaking ability and overall fluency.

Furthermore, listening for specific information such as idioms or cultural references provides an insight into the people and culture associated with the target language. This understanding fosters meaningful communication and connection. For instance, in a language learning class, noting the instructor's use of common expressions and cultural anecdotes can significantly enhance comprehension and engagement with the material, leading to a richer and more immersive learning experience.

Effectively catching details in listening requires a focus on **both verbal and nonverbal messages** while avoiding distractions. Active listening and note-taking are key strategies for accurately grasping details and improving overall comprehension.

Listening Practice

Section A

Introduction to the listening material: Dr. Craig, a clinical psychologist at Mayo Clinic, discusses depression and aims to help people understand its basics. It is a mood disorder that leads to persistent feelings of sadness which can be caused by a combination of factors. The disorder is common, serious, and painful, but it is treatable.

Glossary

Study the words and phrases in the glossary, especially the unfamiliar ones. Do you know how to pronounce or use them in sentences? Use a dictionary to find out more information if necessary.

Words

alleviate	*v.*	to make something less severe 减轻；缓和，缓解
antidepressant	*n.*	a drug used to treat depression 抗抑郁药
apathetic	*adj.*	showing no interest or enthusiasm 冷漠的，淡漠的
appetite	*n.*	physical desire for food 食欲；胃口
approximately	*adv.*	close to a particular number or time although not exactly that number or time 大概；大约；约莫
diabetes	*n.*	a medical condition caused by a lack of insulin, which makes the patient produce a lot of urine and feel very thirsty 糖尿病
diagnosis	*n.*	the act of discovering or identifying the exact cause of an illness or a problem 诊断
disrupt	*v.*	to make it difficult for something to continue in the normal way 扰乱；使中断
down	*adj.*	sad or depressed 悲哀的；沮丧的；情绪低落的
episode	*n.*	an event, a situation, or a period of time in somebody's life, a novel, etc. that is important or interesting in some way（人生的）一段经历；（小说的）片段，插曲
flaw	*n.*	a fault or weakness in a person's character 缺陷；瑕疵
hesitant	*adj.*	slow to speak or act because you feel uncertain, embarrassed or unwilling 犹豫的；踌躇的；不情愿的
hormonal	*adj.*	relating to or involving hormones 荷尔蒙的

56

Unit 4
Depression

irritable	*adj.*	easily annoyed 易怒的
lifespan	*n.*	the length of time that something is likely to live, continue or function 寿命
medication	*n.*	a drug or another form of medicine that you take to prevent or to treat an illness 药剂；药物
menopause	*n.*	the time during which a woman gradually stops menstruating 绝经期；（妇女的）更年期
neurotransmitter	*n.*	a chemical that carries messages from nerve cells to other nerve cells or muscles 神经递质
option	*n.*	something that you can choose to have or do; the freedom to choose what you do 可选择的事物
pregnancy	*n.*	the state of being pregnant 妊娠
serotonin	*n.*	a chemical in the brain that affects how messages are sent from the brain to the body, and also affects how a person feels 血清素，五羟色胺（神经递质，亦影响情绪等）
stigma	*n.*	feelings of disapproval that people have about particular illnesses or ways of behaving 耻辱；羞耻
thyroid	*n.*	an organ in the neck that produces substances that the body needs in order to control the behavior and the way that the body grows 甲状腺
traumatic	*adj.*	extremely unpleasant and causing you to feel upset and/or anxious 痛苦的；极不愉快的
vulnerability	*n.*	the state of being susceptible to physical harm or damage 易受伤害性；脆弱性
withdraw	*v.*	to become quieter and spend less time with other people 脱离（社会）；不与人交往

Phrases

be hard on	to treat one overly strictly or harshly 对……苛刻，严厉

pull back	to withdraw or reduce one's involvement 回撤，退缩
slow down	to become less active or effective 减缓，慢下来
snap out of	to suddenly recover or be freed from some negative or undesirable condition, emotion, or situation 迅速从……中恢复过来 / 摆脱出来

Task 1   Analytical Listening

Watch the video for the first time and complete the following table with information about the definition, symptoms, causes, treatments, and diagnosis of depression.

Understanding Depression—Symptoms, Causes & Treatments

Main Points	Explanation
Definition of depression	It is a mood disorder that (1) _____.
Symptoms of depression	– Emotionally, (2) _____; – Physically, (3) _____, feeling hopeless and helpless; – Behaviorally, (4) _____.
Causes of depression	– Biologically, the causes (5) _____; – Socially, (6) _____, and a lack of social support all contribute to depression risk; – Psychologically, negative thoughts and (7) _____ are possible causes.
Treatments of depression	– Firstly, (8) _____ are an important step; – (9) _____ can help alleviate depressive symptoms; – Finally, (10) _____ can teach us skills to better manage negative thoughts and improve coping behaviors to help break us out of cycles of depression.

(Continued)

Main Points	Explanation
Diagnosis of depression	To diagnose depression, (11) _____ may be used. The result of the diagnosis will help (12) _____ that best fit our situation.

Task 2 Detailed Listening

1. Watch the video clips and fill in the blanks with the details concerned.

1) People tend to keep depression a secret as there is a lot of _____.

2) Depression is different from being in a bad mood in that people suffering from depression _____.

3) Some depression symptoms include _____ thoughts and _____ sleep.

4) It is not easy to diagnose depression as some of its symptoms _____ _____.

5) Neurotransmitters, such as serotonin, can play an important role in regulating bodily functions, such as _____.

2. Do the following statements agree with the information given in the talk? Watch the video again and then decide whether they are

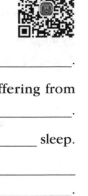

T (true) if the statement agrees with the information, or

F (false) if the statement contradicts the information.

_____ 1) Depression means a bad mood which may last for a short time.

_____ 2) Depression affects the poor more than the rich.

_____ 3) Depression is common and one in six people will experience it in their life.

_____ 4) The emotional, physical, and behavioral symptoms of depression are similar for everyone.

_____ 5) Depression tends to be caused by a combination of various factors according to most experts.

_____ 6) Poverty can contribute to depression risk.

_____ 7) People with depression can mainly deal with the disease by themselves now since there are some effective medications and helpful guidelines.

_____ 8) People affected by depression can also seek help from family members or friends.

Task 3 Critical Listening

Watch the video for the third time and discuss the following questions with your language partner.

1) What are the possible social causes of college students' mental problems (such as depression and anxiety) in our society? How should they deal with them?

2) What attitudes do people have towards mental problems in their life? Interpret them from your point of view.

Section B

Introduction to the listening material: In the video from BBC News, James Longman talks about his father and grandfather, and wonders whether he has inherited any mental health problems. He learns that mental illnesses are caused by a collection of genes rather than a single gene, and inherited illnesses can vary in individuals.

Glossary

Study the words and phrases in the glossary, especially the unfamiliar ones. Do you know how to pronounce or use them in sentences? Use a dictionary to find out more information if necessary.

Words

blazer	n.	a jacket often showing the colors or badge of a club, school, team, etc.（常带有俱乐部、学校、运动队等的颜色或徽章的）夹克
bout	n.	a short period during which there is a lot of a particular thing, usually something unpleasant 一阵；一通（尤指坏事）

cherish	v.	to keep an idea, a hope or a pleasant feeling in your mind for a long time 怀念；抱有（信念、希望）；怀有（好感）
essentially	adv.	basically, fundamentally 本质上；根本上；基本上
giveaway	n.	a thing that makes an unintentional revelation 使真相暴露的事物
grave	n.	a place in the ground where a dead person is buried 坟墓
guilt	n.	the unhappy feelings caused by knowing or thinking that you have done something wrong 内疚；悔恨
highlight	v.	to emphasize something, especially so that people give it more attention 突出；强调
inherit	v.	to have qualities, physical features, etc. that are similar to those of your parents, grandparents, etc. 经遗传获得
low	n.	a very difficult time in somebody's life or career 艰难时期，低谷
matron	n.	a woman who works as a nurse in a school（学校的）女舍监
MRI	abbr.	magnetic resonance imaging 磁共振成像
nurture	n.	care, encouragement and support given to someone while he or she is growing 养育；培养
psychiatrist	n.	a doctor who studies and treats mental illnesses 精神病学家；精神科医生
punch	v.	to hit with a sharp blow of the fist 拳打
reversible	adj.	that can be changed so that something returns to its original state or situation 可逆的；可医治的
strand	n.	a single thin piece of thread, wire, hair, etc. 股，缕
swing	v.	to move backward or forward or from side to side while hanging from a fixed point; to make something do this （使）摆动，摇摆，摇荡
thermometer	n.	an instrument used for measuring the temperature 温度计
trigger	n.	something that is the cause of a particular reaction or development, especially a bad one（尤指引发不良反应或发展的）起因，诱因

upbringing	*n.*	the way in which a child is cared for and taught how to behave while he or she is growing up 抚育；培养
weird	*adj.*	strange or unusual and difficult to explain 奇异的；不寻常的；怪诞的

Phrases

at the crux	at the critical point 处在关键时期
burst into sobs	to suddenly weep with convulsive gasps 突然抽泣起来
give access to	to grant one to have the permission, means, or ability to use or reach someone or something 向……开放
think away	to use one's thoughts to eliminate or overcome negative thoughts or emotions 通过专注来消除不良想法或情绪

Task 1 Analytical Listening

Watch the video for the first time and find the details for the main points of the speech.

Did I Inherit Mental Illness?

Main Points	Supporting Details
The origin of James' worry	(1) _____.
Johnny and Lucy's worry	(2) _____.
James' attitude towards his father	(3) _____.
The relation between genes and mental diseases	(4) _____.
The way to mitigate the consequences of genetic inheritance	(5) _____.

Unit 4 Depression

Task 2 Detailed Listening

Watch the video clips and answer the questions with details concerned.

1) What did James' father look like?

2) James says "That's a kind of Catch-22" when talking about his father. What does he mean?

3) Johnny has bipolar disorder while Lucy is free from it though they are twins. Explain the reason for the difference.

4) According to James' investigation, if a parent has bipolar disorder, what is the possibility for the child to have it?

5) What is Lucy's attitude towards her family's mental illness and having their own children?

6) What was James' feeling when he discovered his father committed suicide by setting fire to the flat and jumping out of the window?

7) How can the changes in the brains of people at risk of depression be reversed?

8) What is Ann's reaction to her husband's death?

Task 3 Critical Listening

Watch the video again and discuss the following questions with your language partner.

1) Should mentally ill people get married? Why or why not?

2) How can we minimize the consequences of mental illness?

Speech Workshop

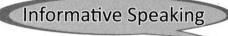

In general, academic speeches are delivered to achieve two primary goals: to inform or to persuade the audience. This unit focuses on how to construct and present a competent informative speech.

An **informative speech** is to provide the audience with new information or clarify confusion or misunderstanding about a topic. It falls into five categories in terms of subjects: **things, people, events, processes, and concepts**.

- **Things:** Speeches may focus on tangible things that can be perceived with the senses. These can include places like the Great Wall of China or Paris, substances like charcoal or soil, objects like guitars or cars, or health issues like depression or anxiety.

- **People:** Speeches about people often explore their lives or actions and what they teach us about being human. The subject can be well-known, such as a film star or athlete, or less known, such as a friend or family member.

- **Events:** Speeches may focus on significant historical or contemporary events, such as the Industrial Revolution or the Renaissance.

- **Processes:** Speeches on a process explain how something works, is made, or is done. Examples include driving a car, assembling a computer, or cooking pudding.

- **Concepts:** Finally, speeches may focus on concepts about an idea, belief, principle, or theory, which are abstract or general, such as independence and freedom.

The following discussion of informative speaking strategies will cover the selection of topics, creation of purpose statements, and organization of an informative speech.

Selecting a Topic

The topic for an informative speech should interest both the audience and the speaker. With vast information available online, the goal of public speaking isn't to "dump data" but to present information in an **intellectually stimulating** way. Engaging or useful information can captivate the audience and allow the speaker to speak with genuine passion, making it easier to engage listeners and make an impact.

Drafting a Purpose Statement

After selecting a topic, the speaker should develop a specific purpose statement, which outlines what the audience should learn from the speech. Here are some examples of informative speech purpose statements:

- To inform the audience about different kinds of Chinese tea.
- To inform the audience about the historical significance of the French Revolution.
- To inform the audience about how to cook Yorkshire pudding.

In the body of the speech, the main points will be elaborated based on the purpose.

Organizing a Speech

It is crucial to ensure that a speech has a clear and easy-to-follow structure since the audience cannot re-listen to parts they miss. This differs from reading an essay where they can stop and re-read. Like any other speech, an informative speech can be divided into three sections: introduction, body, and conclusion.

- **Introduction:** This section should grab the audience's interest and orient them to the topic of the speech. Typically, it includes a credibility statement to establish the speaker's authority, a thesis statement summarizing the main point, and a preview of the key points to outline the speech's structure.

- **Body:** The body section provides the audience with all the information they will need to understand the topic. Typically, it includes three or more main points organized in a structure appropriate to the topic and thesis supported by examples or evidence. It is important to consider time constraints here. For example, if there are only three minutes to speak, attempting to develop four or more points would be too ambitious.

- **Conclusion:** This short section reinforces the thesis, summarizes the main points, and encourages the audience to reflect on the message of the speech, providing a sense of closure.

Organizational Patterns for the Body Section

Several organizational patterns are typically used for an informative speech:

- **Topical:** This pattern organizes the main points by distinct topics. It is versatile and works well when the main points are distinct. For example, a speech on the typical challenges faced by freshmen on campus can use a topical pattern.

- **Spatial:** This pattern is useful for describing a place. For example, a speech on how to tour the Forbidden City can be organized spatially.

- **Chronological:** This pattern follows a time order and is ideal for explaining sequences of events. A speech on how to lose weight in three stages can be structured chronologically.

- **Comparative:** This pattern is used to explain the similarities and differences between two or more things. A speech introducing Egyptian and Mexican pyramids can be given in this way.

- **Causal:** It is used to explain cause/effect relationships. Typically, with this pattern, there are two main points: one focused on the causes of an event, the other on its effects. A speech on water pollution can be organized causally.

With a purpose statement, main ideas, and an organizational pattern in place, the next step is to develop the speech with supporting details.

Task 1   Pair Work: Listen and Share

Listen to the speech given by Dr. Craig about depression (Section A), and take notes to identify the purpose statement and the organizational pattern used. Then discuss your findings with your language partner to improve your notes.

Task 2   Unit Project

Compose a 3-minute informative speech on a meaningful topic. You might tell a story about yourself, your family, or a group of people. Alternatively, you could focus on a specific organization or place, such as Tsinghua University. Your speech could also explore themes like beliefs, ideas, or growing up. Whatever topic you choose, ensure your speech has a clear purpose and is well-organized.

Pronunciation Workshop

Loss of Plosion

Loss of plosion is a kind of elision in English pronunciation. **Elision** is the omission of one or more phonemes usually in order to simplify the pronunciation, which is characteristic of rapid, colloquial speech in English.

Elision of vowels is likely to take place, especially in a sequence of unstressed syllables in respect of /ə/. Weak vowels are more susceptible to elision after plosives /p/, /t/, /k/. For example, in "temperature" /tempərɪtʃə/ → /temprɪtʃə/, /ə/ after /p/ is elided. It is the same case in examples of "police", "history", and "interesting". It also occurs in weak vowels before /n/, /l/, and /r/.

Elision is much more common for consonants though it occurs for both vowels and consonants. Some consonants are elided when they occur in certain contexts. For example, the dropping of the initial /h/ occurs in unstressed pronouns—as in "give him", /gɪvɪm/ or "tell him", /telɪm/, or forms of the auxiliary "have"—as in "would have", /wʊdəv/, "should have", /ʃʊdəv/, etc.

Unit 4
Depression

This unit chooses to focus on one consonant elision, namely, the loss of plosive sounds which frequently occurs in spoken language.

Plosive consonants are made by completely blocking the flow of air as it leaves the body, which is followed by releasing the air. There are six plosive phonemes in English pronunciation: /p/, /b/, /t/, /d/, /k/, /g/. The sounds /b/, /d/, /g/ are voiced; they are pronounced with vibration in the vocal cords. /p/, /t/, /k/ are voiceless and they are produced with a puff of air (aspirating) in English pronunciation.

The plosive consonants in English may be unexploded when they occur before another plosive or most of the other consonants, as in "rea<u>c</u>t", "prom<u>p</u>t", "si<u>t</u> down", and "nex<u>t</u> morning", where the plosion of /k/, /p/, and /t/ is not released.

Loss of plosion is a natural process of language change that occurs in many languages. Its general function is to make speech more fluid and easier to pronounce as it allows speakers to reduce the muscular effort involved in pronouncing consonant sounds, particularly in rapid or continuous speech.

Task 1   Sample Analysis

Listen to the recording of the following phrases and sentences. Pay attention to the loss of plosion (underlined). Then practice reading them.

1) ta<u>ke c</u>are / trie<u>d t</u>o / tha<u>t d</u>ay

2) a fa<u>t b</u>oy / a blac<u>k c</u>at / sto<u>p t</u>alking / a re<u>d b</u>anner

3) a har<u>d t</u>ime / knoc<u>k d</u>own / won'<u>t d</u>o / the bes<u>t d</u>octor

4) rea<u>d t</u>hat / sai<u>d t</u>he man / the righ<u>t t</u>hing / a shor<u>t v</u>illage

5) swee<u>t f</u>ruit / sto<u>p t</u>hat noise / a bi<u>g c</u>hange / a blac<u>k ch</u>air

6) some ri<u>pe c</u>herries / a goo<u>d d</u>octor / ru<u>b g</u>ently / don'<u>t k</u>now

7) las<u>t n</u>ight / lou<u>d n</u>oise / hel<u>p m</u>e / nex<u>t m</u>orning / a clu<u>b m</u>ember

8) <u>We'd better get there</u> in time.

9) I <u>knocked them</u> off the desk.

10) He <u>didn't turn</u> up though he <u>had promised</u> to come.

Task 2   Listen and Identify: Loss of Plosion

Listen to the following conversation about mental health consultation provided by Tina Yun, an English lecturer at Tsinghua University. Try to identify the places where the loss of plosion occurs and mark them.

S = Student who hasn't been himself lately

C = Counselor (Therapist)

C: First of all, how are you feeling today? What brings you here?

S: I don't know. Life's been a mess. It's hard to talk about.

C: I understand. Any stressors in your life?

S: Well, I used to be a top student. I mean, I got top marks. I didn't even have to study that hard. But since entering this school, I've found that the work has gotten a lot more difficult. My high school was a relatively good school, but it didn't prepare me well for what I'm doing now. I want to get a 4.0 this semester, but the course load is just out of my control.

C: You have a lot more control over your life than you think. A 4.0 seems like a big goal for now, but it can be more attainable if you break it down into baby steps.

S: How would that look?

C: You could start by making a list of what you need to get done every day. I suggest you start with smaller goals that you know you'll be able to complete. There's no need to stress yourself out by stretching yourself too much, at least not for now.

S: I've tried doing that, but even when I set aside time for studying I find my mind drifting off.

C: What do you think about?

S: Lots of things. I worry a lot. For one thing, my parents will be very disappointed when they find out about my grades. I think I might fail my design course and I'm barely getting by in my other courses. And it's not just that I might flunk out of college. I got a full scholarship to a less competitive school but I convinced my parents to let me come here instead. They had to sacrifice a lot for my tuition.

C: The semester isn't even halfway over yet. You still have at least the midterm and the final to pull your grades up. You can start now. If you want a 4.0, go for it!

S: Yeah, I guess so. I guess if I flunk out my Plan B would be—

C: [Laughs]

S: What's so funny?

C: I just think it's funny how little confidence you have. Don't think of a Plan B. That will make you lose focus. Just focus on one plan.

S: I'll try that out. Also, I'm afraid that other people will laugh at me for aiming so high or trying so hard.

C: Then whose problem is it?

S: Not mine.

C: Great. Anything else bothering you?

S: Yes, I look at social media during my study breaks and I find myself comparing. It makes me feel like I'm so insecure. Occasionally I get a temporary ego boost but ultimately it just leaves me feeling empty. I know it's just a waste of time, and I still think of it when I'm supposed to be studying after break time.

C: What do you compare?

S: I know this sounds stupid and this is very embarrassing for me to admit, but I compare looks. It started when a friend told me she felt ugly. Afterwards I noticed on social media that a lot of people look better than myself. I once tried talking to another friend about it and she just told me I was stupid for objectifying myself. Some days I feel very unattractive and worry that I may never find a partner.

C: Your friend sounds insensitive. Also, there's a difference between feeling ugly and being ugly. A lot of times, feeling ugly has to do more with perception than reality. I have an assignment for you this week. Check out the people around you when you're out in public, the people whose appearances haven't been photoshopped. In your head make a note of whether the people you find less attractive really are all by themselves. You might be surprised. What else do you want to talk about?

S: Well, I hang out with a lot of people. There's a group of 10 people who I hang out with regularly. We have lunch for two hours together every day, and I also go to club meetings with some of them in the evenings. It sounds great and all, but the truth is that after we see each other I immediately start feeling very lonely. I actually don't really enjoy their company, but I'm terrified of being alone.

C: Sounds like you need to find something you're passionate about. You said you go to club meetings. What do you do there? Could those interests be developed into long-time hobbies?

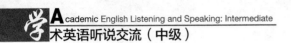

S: Actually, I'm not into any of those clubs. I joined them only because a couple of my friends were interested, and they asked me to come along. There's also a knitting club that I think might be fun, but I've never gone to a meeting.

C: What's keeping you from checking it out?

S: All my friends are either unavailable for the meetings or are uninterested.

C: Try going anyway. You might find a new passion and new friends.

S: Sure.

C: And our time is up for today. Let's schedule for next week at the same time?

S: Sounds good. Thank you, and see you next week.

Supplementary Materials

1. A speech—"How to Recover from Depression"

2. A documentary—"Mental Health"

3. A conversation—"The Secret to Ending Mental Illness"

Unit 5

Language Learning

1. "A different language is a different vision of life."

—Federico Fellini (1920–1993), Italian filmmaker

2. "If you talk to a man in a language he understands, that goes to his head. If you talk to him in his language, that goes to his heart."

— Nelson Mandela (1918–2013), South African anti-apartheid activist and politician

Lead-in

Learning a new language is a valuable and rewarding experience that can open up new opportunities and perspectives. It enables communication with people from different cultures and enhances cognitive abilities or career prospects. However, mastering a foreign language can also be challenging. Which new languages have you ever learned? And what have you gained from learning them? Have you come across any difficulties? What are your tips for new learners? Please review the expressions from the Preparing to Speak box and use them in discussion with your classmates.

Preparing to Speak

Match the words and phrases with their definitions.

1. confidence
2. embarrassment
3. linguistic performance
4. lingua franca
5. identity
6. ineffective
7. interaction
8. linguistic competence
9. native
10. drill

a. the distinguishing character or personality of an individual
b. not producing any significant effect or result
c. the activity of being with and talking to other people
d. the belief that you are able to do things well
e. belonging to a place by birth or origin
f. a feeling of self-consciousness, shame, or awkwardness
g. an activity that practices a particular skill and often involves repeating the same thing several times
h. the ability to produce and comprehend sentences in a language
i. a language used for communication between groups of people who speak different languages
j. the unconscious knowledge of grammar that allows a speaker to use and understand a language

Learning Objectives

This unit will help you to explore the benefits of learning a new language and provide tips and strategies to make the language learning experience more effective and enjoyable. Upon completion of this unit, you will be able to

√ understand the importance of learning new languages and how to learn a new language effectively;

Unit 5
Language Learning

> √ apply signal words appropriately in speaking;
>
> √ identify word stress and sentence stress in pronunciation;
>
> √ analyze and apply strategies for composing a persuasive speech.

Listening Focus

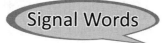

When listening to an English speech, listeners do not allocate equal attention to every word. Instead, they adopt a selective listening strategy, focusing more on essential words. This method offers greater flexibility, aiding comprehension of the main points even when encountering unfamiliar terms.

Signal words or **transition words** play a critical role in communication. Their primary function is to assist listeners in understanding the direction of the conversation, the relation between the ideas, and the significance of each idea. When listening to a speech, these words also clarify its organization, guiding listeners through the discourse by indicating its structure and progression. Essentially, signal words act as navigational aids, helping listeners follow the flow of the conversation or speech and understand the information presented.

There are various types of signal words used in conversations or speeches which can:

- mark the beginning or end of a speech or conversation;
- signal changes or return to previous topics;
- establish logical connections between ideas, such as cause and effect, parts and wholes, relative importance, addition, and comparison/contrast.

The following words and phrases serve to indicate transitions and help cue listeners about the logical connections between ideas.

Table 5.1 A list of signal words and phrases

Begin a topic	to begin with; to start off; firstly; that reminds me; I need to talk to you about; Let us start with; I just thought of; speaking of; I was going to tell you about

(Continued)

End a topic		in short; to recap; on the whole; overall; in brief; That is it for today; It was nice talking to you; Well, that is all I have to say; Does anyone have any questions?; Is that all?
Return to a previous topic		just to get back to…; about that…; I just remembered; to return to what I was saying
Connect ideas in a talk	reasons	because; since; for this reason
	results	as a result; so; therefore; thus; consequently; accordingly
	examples	for example; for instance; such as; like; take the case of; to demonstrate
	comparisons	similarly; correspondingly; likewise; equally; like; in the same way; at the same time
	contrasts or contradiction	in contrast; on the other hand; unlike; on the contrary; differing from; but; however; actually; yet; conversely; still; while; whereas
	concession	admittedly; after all; all the same; although; clearly; it is true (that); in spite of; nevertheless; of course; even if/though; no matter how/what/where/when
	addition	furthermore; moreover; besides; additionally; also; indeed; in fact; not only…but also
	sequence	first; second; third; next; before; afterwards; finally
	clarification	in other words; that is to say; specifically; namely; actually; more precisely

Listening Practice

Section A

Introduction to the listening material: This video speech from Ouino Languages expounds on the benefits of learning a new language with interesting examples and convincing facts. Besides elementary communication, a new language allows for the expression of emotions, deeper connections between people, acquiring broader horizons, and even improved brain health.

Unit 5 Language Learning

Glossary

Study the words and phrases in the glossary, especially the unfamiliar ones. Do you know how to pronounce or use them in sentences? Use a dictionary to find out more information if necessary.

Words

access	*n.*	the right or opportunity to use or benefit from something 机会，通道
Alzheimer's	*n.*	a progressive disease beginning with mild memory loss possibly leading to a loss of the ability to carry on a conversation and respond to the environment 阿尔茨海默病；老年痴呆症
bilingualism	*n.*	the ability to speak two languages fluently 双语能力
bubble	*n.*	a zone of cognitive or psychological isolation, in which one's preexisting ideas are reinforced through interactions with like-minded people or those with similar social identities 安全之地，世外桃源
dementia	*n.*	a medical condition that especially affects old people, causing memory and other mental abilities to gradually become worse, and leading to confused behavior 痴呆，失智症
density	*n.*	the degree to which something has a high mass 密度
clip	*n.*	a short part of a film/movie that is shown separately 一段（视频）
darn	*adj.*	used to emphasize what is said 非常的
earpiece	*n.*	part of hearing aid that fits in or is held next to the ear 耳机
grateful	*adj.*	feeling or showing thanks 感激的
maintenance	*n.*	the act of keeping something in good condition by checking or repairing it regularly 维持；保养

nonverbal	*adj.*	not using words 非语言的
perspective	*n.*	a particular attitude towards something; a way of thinking about something 态度；观点；思考方法
post	*n.*	something (such as a message) that is published online 帖子，留言信息
prospect	*n.*	the possibility that something will happen 前景，可能性
résumé	*n.*	a short summary or account of something 简历
sarcasm	*n.*	a way of using words that are the opposite of what you mean in order to be unpleasant to somebody or to make fun of them 讽刺，挖苦
scan	*n.*	a medical test in which a machine produces a picture of the inside of a person's body on a computer screen after taking X-rays 扫描
spontaneity	*n.*	the quality or state of being natural and unconstrained 自然性
stroke	*n.*	a sudden serious illness when a blood vessel in the brain bursts or is blocked 中风

Phrases

cerebral cortex	the furrowed outer layer of gray matter in the front part of the brain 大脑皮层
a pain in the butt	someone or something that is very annoying 令人讨厌的人/事

Task 1 Analytical Listening

Watch the video for the first time and complete the following summary of the speech.

Unit 5
Language Learning

Why Is It Necessary to Learn a Foreign Language?

Some people think learning new languages (1) _____ in the future as English is now serving as a global language. In addition, translation technology can help overcome the obstacles of foreign languages.

However, translation technology cannot really replace human interactions. Languages are more than elementary communication, the part that can practically be translated. A great percentage of our communication is nonverbal. Features of human interactions such as (2) _____ cannot be well conveyed by machines. That is why jokes told by a computer are not really funny. Finally, due to (3) _____, there will always be some important delay in translation, which makes communication an unpleasant experience.

The language we speak is part of who we are. It is well exemplified by Will Smith's performance in a TV show. Despite his clumsy Spanish speaking, he received crazy responses from the Spanish-speaking audience, as he used the new language to (4) _____.

Besides its "connection" function, a new language can (5) _____ _____. Speaking a new language is obviously a challenge to anyone which will be a great add-on to our résumé. It will also enable us to meet more clients and to build business relationships internationally.

In addition to our job, learning new languages can even (6) _____. Studies indicate that bilingualism can help improve people's memory, attention, and decision-making abilities. It can even delay dementia and improve the ability to recover from a stroke.

Finally, a new language leads us out of our own zone of life and into a different world of culture, works of art and people. This will add to our mind new points of view, more perspectives on things, help us better understand our own culture and language. In conclusion, it can (7) _____.

Task 2 Detailed Listening

1. Watch the video again and fill in the blanks with signal words or phrases from the speech. A hint as to the function of each answer is given in the brackets.

1) Using translation technology is a more or less annoying thing _____ it is an impressive and helpful quick travel tool. (concession)

2) Will Smith cannot speak much Spanish; _____ the Spanish speakers go crazy when he makes an effort to speak the language for them. (contrast)

3) When we use simple words _____ "hello" and "thank you" in the local language, it is easy to get connected with the locals in a more personal way. (example)

4) Learning a new language is seen as a difficult task to accomplish and is _____ _____ a great add-on to any résumé. (result)

5) Research indicates bilingualism can help improve people's memory and attention; it can _____ improve the ability to recover from a stroke. (addition)

2. Watch the video clips and fill in the blanks with words or phrases you hear from the speech.

1) To illustrate that human interaction is irreplaceable, the speaker uses the research results showing that the actual words we speak are only 7%, and 38% of communication is _____.

2) When we say "your language is who you are", it contains your _____ _____.

3) Speaking new languages will open up more doors for jobs to us as it will allow us to interact with _____ and participate in _____.

4) Bilingualism can change our brains, as brain scans have shown a greater _____ _____ in the cerebral cortex and a better _____ during aging.

5) Learning a new language will enable us to get access to its culture and view the world from a new point of view which gives us _____.

Task 3 Critical Listening

Watch the video for the third time and discuss the following questions with your language partner.

1) With the progress of AI research, translation technology produces results that are very close to human translation. Do you believe AI will sooner or later replace human translation and even replace human interaction?

2) As illustrated in this video speech, learning foreign languages can benefit us in various aspects. However, there are still people who insist that learning new languages is not necessary and it is a waste of time and energy. What is your point of view?

Section B

Introduction to the listening material: The TED speaker, Marianna Pascal, emphasizes that it is important for non-native English learners to focus on their interlocutors and the outcomes of their interactions. She argues that this approach can build confidence and lead to successful English communication.

Glossary

Study the words and phrases in the glossary, especially the unfamiliar ones. Do you know how to pronounce or use them in sentences? Use a dictionary to find out more information if necessary.

Words

clarity	n.	the quality of being expressed clearly 清晰；清楚；明确
disgusting	adj.	extremely unpleasant 极糟的；令人不快的
gross	adj.	very unpleasant 令人不快的，使人厌恶的
lousy	adj.	(informal) very bad 非常糟的
multitask	v.	to do several things at the same time 同时做数件事情
self-awareness	n.	the quality of being conscious of one's own feelings, character, etc. 自我意识
similarity	n.	the state of being like something 相像性；相仿性；类似性
smelly	adj.	having an unpleasant smell 有难闻气味的；有臭味的
supervisor	n.	a person who is in charge of a particular department or unit 主管人；监督
symptom	n.	a sign that something exists, especially something bad 征候；征兆

Phrases

as good as it gets	used to say that nothing better is possible or available 再无更好的了
cyber café	a café where people can pay to use the Internet 网吧
sales rep	a person employed to represent a business and to sell its merchandise 销售代表，推销员
screw up	to cause to act or function in a crazy or confused way 弄得很糟
shut down	to cease to operate or cause to cease to operate 停工，关闭
tons of	a very large amount of (things or people) 非常多的（东西或人）

Task 1 Analytical Listening

Watch the video for the first time and complete the following table with main points and their supporting details from the speech.

Learning a Language—Speak It like You're Playing a Video Game

Main Points	Supporting Details
There are two similarities between many Malaysians' attitude towards English and Marianna's daughter's attitude towards practicing piano.	They were afraid of (1) _____. They were (2) _____.
Faizal and the game player shared (3) _____.	The lousy game player focused on the game he was playing with no embarrassment; Faizal focused on the person he was speaking to with no thoughts about his own mistakes.
The low-level English speaker in the pharmacy was more (4) _____ than the high-level speaker.	The low-level speaker focused on the person she was talking to and getting a result; the high-level speaker (5) _____.

Unit 5 Language Learning

(Continued)

Main Points	Supporting Details
(6) _____ is very important for non-native speakers like Malaysians.	Most of English conversations now involve non-native speakers, and English is largely non-native speakers' language in a sense; the language is still taught ineffectively like an art at school and students are judged more on correctness than on clarity.
Why is the attitude developed in school about focusing on language correctness not appropriate?	For non-native speakers, multitasking, getting the desired result from the speech and speaking correctly, may (7) _____ _____.

Task 2 Detailed Listening

1. Watch the video clips and complete the following sentences with signal words from the speech and tell what relations they indicate.

1) The speaker claims that a person's ability of communication in English _____ has very little to do with their English level.

   Relation: _____

2) Her daughter dreaded going to piano lessons; _____ a lot of Malaysians went into English conversations with the same sort of feeling of dread.

   Relation: _____

3) A lot of piano students are afraid of practicing _____ their success is measured by how few mistakes they make.

   Relation: _____

4) I could see the reasons for many people's hate of English, _____ I still couldn't figure out people like Faizal could be so different and successful in communication in English.

   Relation: _____

5) There was no embarrassment or shyness _____ the game player's performance was terrible.

   Relation: _____

6) The sales rep in the pharmacy spoke English _____ playing piano as my daughter did.

                                                          Relation: _____

7) When I walked to the girl whose English is at a low level, there was no fear. _____ she was just looking at me.

                                                          Relation: _____

2. Watch the video again and choose the best answer from the four choices marked A), B), C) and D).

1) From her experience of teaching English to people in southeast Asia, the speaker has discovered that _____.
   A) the higher their English level is, the better they can communicate
   B) the lower their English level is, the better they can communicate
   C) how well they can communicate in English has very little to do with their English level
   D) how well they can communicate in English has little to do with their attitude towards English

2) One of the things the speaker wants to share with us is _____.
   A) how to communicate in English successfully with confidence at a very low level of English like Faizal
   B) how to learn more accurate and formal English in a non-native environment such as Malaysia
   C) learning English is more important to our children than to us
   D) if we want to speak English with calm, clear confidence, we have to forget our mother tongue

3) A lot of Malaysians are short of confidence in English speaking as they _____.
   A) have no idea of what good proper English sounds like and thus have no standard to follow
   B) have the idea of what good proper English sounds like and feel discouraged by their own bad English
   C) are clear that they are in a non-native speaking environment
   D) realize speaking English is like playing the piano which is equally difficult

4) The game player played in the cyber café with no embarrassment though his performance was terrible because _____.
   A) people standing there watching him were his friends
   B) the game was so challenging that few people could play well

C) he was not a shy person

D) he concentrated entirely on the game, paying no attention to other things

5) The sales rep in the pharmacy failed to communicate with me in English because _____.

A) she spoke too fast and walked in circles so that I could not follow her

B) she could not tell the difference between DHA and EPA

C) she concentrated too much on her own speaking to take care of my need

D) she spoke English with so many technical terms that I could not understand her

6) When non-native English speakers are in a stressful situation of keeping both language correctness and clarity in mind, _____.

A) the efficiency of communication will be greatly improved

B) they cannot understand or express themselves well as the brain multitasks

C) their language quality will be improved while clarity will suffer

D) their language clarity will be improved while correctness will suffer

Task 3 Critical Listening

Watch the video for the third time and discuss the following questions with your language partner.

1) Marianna Pascal's speech emphasizes the importance of focusing on the outcome of communication rather than the quality of language used. Do you agree with this perspective? Please explain your point of view.

2) The speaker encourages us to focus on the person we are talking to instead of on ourselves for more effective communication. Besides this, do you have any more tips for effective communication in English?

Speech Workshop

Persuasive Speaking

Persuasive speaking aims to influence the beliefs, attitudes, values, or behaviors of the audience through reasoning and argument. This unit delves into the core elements of persuasive speaking, encompassing the selection of compelling topics, the formulation of propositions, the organization of speech ideas, and essential persuasive strategies.

Choosing a Persuasive Speech Topic

Effective persuasive speech topics are current, controversial, and significant for society. Such topics engage the audience more deeply when they resonate with both the speaker and the broader community. However, being provocative without reason or choosing extremist topics can harm the speaker's credibility and undermine the speech goals.

Determining a Proposition

A proposition serves as the guiding principle for a speech, shaping its content to align with the overall objective. Persuasive speeches are typically classified into three categories based on their propositions: fact, value, or policy.

- **Propositions of fact** focus on establishing the truth or falsehood of a claim through logical arguments and objective evidence.

- **Propositions of value** delve into discussions of what is morally right or wrong, good or bad, often evoking emotional responses and supported by expert testimony.

- **Propositions of policy** advocate for specific actions or changes, necessitating research into existing laws, procedures, and current legislative considerations.

For example, considering solar energy:

- Proposition of fact: The adoption of solar energy has surged dramatically over the past decade, establishing it as a leading and sustainable energy source for the future.

- Proposition of value: Investing in solar energy infrastructure is essential for promoting environmental sustainability and reducing carbon emissions for future generations.

- Proposition of policy: Governments should provide more subsidies to promote the use of solar energy.

Organizing a Persuasive Speech

In general, a persuasive speech is structured like an informative speech with an introduction, a body part, and a conclusion. However, its primary goal is to advocate for a specific viewpoint or action. Persuasive speeches can be structured using various effective patterns, among which the typical ones include problem-solution, cause-effect, and comparison-advantage.

- **The problem-solution pattern** is ideal for policy change arguments. For example, "The high levels of plastic waste in oceans can be addressed by banning single-use plastics. A more elaborate variation of the problem-solution pattern focusing on motivational appeals is known as **Monroe's Motivated Sequence**[1]. It uses five steps: get attention, establish the need, satisfy the need, visualize the future, and call for action."

- **The cause-effect pattern** is useful for discussing the consequences of actions. For example, "Implementing stricter emissions regulations can significantly reduce air pollution."

- **The comparison-advantage pattern** compares options to highlight the superior choice. For example, "Public transportation is a superior solution to personal cars in alleviating traffic congestion."

Essential Strategies

To enhance the persuasive power of a speech, three essential strategies are often employed: ethical appeal (ethos), emotional appeal (pathos), and logical appeal (logos).

- **Ethical appeal:** Ethical appeal means to establish the speaker's credibility or character. It includes the idea of whether the speaker is qualified to speak on the topic, and whether he or she can establish common ground with the audience confidently. It is meant to make the audience believe that the speaker is a credible source and is worth listening to.

- **Emotional appeal:** Emotional appeal means to attempt to persuade an audience by appealing to their emotions. One of the most common ways to bring emotional appeals into a speech is to use memorable examples and stories. Word choices are also important to emotional appeals. Vivid, powerful, and emotion-laden language can be very effective in moving an audience.

- **Logical appeal:** Appealing to logic is to convince an audience by the use of logical arguments. To use logic would be to cite facts and statistics, historical and literary analogies, and credible authorities on a subject.

Understanding and effectively applying these elements and strategies will empower you to craft compelling and impactful persuasive speeches.

---

1 This pattern was proposed by Alan H. Monroe (1903–1975), a Purdue University psychology professor who wrote the book, *Monroe's Principles of Speech*.

Task 1   Pair Work: Listen and Share

Watch the video "Why Is It Necessary to Learn a Foreign Language?" (Section A) and take notes on the attention-getter, proposition, and organizational pattern of the speech. Additionally, identify and discuss with your language partner which persuasive strategies (ethos, pathos, logos) the speaker uses to enhance the power of the speech. After discussing your observations, revise and refine your notes based on the insights gained from your conversation.

Task 2   Unit Project

Compose a 3-minute persuasive speech on language learning with a clear goal and suitable organizational pattern. Try to use some of the strategies introduced in the unit to make your speech powerful.

Pronunciation Workshop

Stress

Stress is a distinct trait of English pronunciation. It involves pronouncing certain syllables or words with more emphasis than others within a word or sentence. While predicting stress patterns isn't entirely reliable, some rules can help determine where stress typically falls in a word or sentence.

Word Stress

In most English words of two syllables, the stress falls on the first syllable, e.g., "worker", "father", "mother", and "daughter". However, there are exceptions. In most two-syllable verbs and prepositions, the stress is on the second syllable, e.g., "believe", "depend", "about", and "inside".

In most English words of three or four syllables, the stress falls on the third syllable from the end, e.g., "family", "elephant", and "informative".

There are usually two degrees of stress marked in dictionaries: primary stress and secondary stress. Owing to the English tendency to alternate stressed and unstressed syllables, the secondary stress will often precede the primary stress by two syllables, e.g., "opportunity" [ˌɒpə'tʃuːnəti], and "entertainment" [ˌentə'teɪnmənt].

Unit 5
Language Learning

In words that carry the following endings, the primary stress falls on the syllable immediately preceding the ending:

-ian: physician, vegetarian, historian, Egyptian

-ic: classic, basic, realistic, electric, scientific, fantastic

-ion: attention, decision, depression, education, promotion

-ience: obedience, resilience, experience

-ient: efficient, obedient, proficient, ingredient

-ious: delicious, nutritious, rebellious, suspicious, victorious

Words that use suffixes like "-ade", "-ee", "-ese", "-eer", "-que", "-ette", or "-oon" have the primary stress actually placed on the suffixes. For example, "brigade", "Crusade", "parade", "employee", "guarantee", "refugee", "Chinese", "Portuguese", "pioneer", "volunteer", "unique", "technique", "cassette", and "cartoon".

With very few exceptions, English compound words are stressed on their first component. Here are some examples: "butterfly", "firework", "moonlight", "newspaper", "pineapple", and "sunflower".

Sentence Stress

Sentence stress or **sentence focus** refers to the kind of stress that falls on certain words that are semantically important. As a general rule, the relative stress of the words in a sentence depends on their relative importance. Main verbs, adverbs, nouns, adjectives, and demonstrative pronouns are content words that are generally considered important and tend to be stressed. Function words including prepositions, articles, and auxiliary verbs are generally unstressed unless the speaker wishes to call special attention to them.

Task 1 Sample Analysis: Word Stress

Find the stress of the following words with the help of a dictionary.

1) apple   2) oppose

3) balance   4) consequence

5) journey   6) magnificent

7) below   8) communication

9) behind   10) profession

11) within   12) engineer

13) detect   14) refugee

15) reveal   16) Japanese

Task 2 Listen and Identify: Sentence Stress

Listen and underline the stressed words. Then read them in the same way.

1) A lot of noise.

2) A waste of time.

3) Just for a while.

4) Give him a call.

5) Lend me a hand.

6) Show me the way.

7) It's hard to say.

8) What about a drink?

9) Try to be on time.

10) Don't be such a fool.

11) It's difficult to learn.

12) You'll see him in a week.

13) She wanted to write to him.

14) You've practiced it perfectly.

Task 3 Listen and Practice: Sentence Stress

Listen to the following conversation about stress provided by Adam Rose, an English lecturer at Tsinghua University. Mark the word(s) that receive(s) the most prominent stress in each sentence. Then practice reading the sentences.

S = Student   T = Teacher

S: Hello, can I ask you to give me some feedback on my presentation?

T: How do you think it went?

S: I spent a long time writing my presentation, making attractive slides, and tried varying my intonation to make it interesting for the other students, but I still felt that a lot of people couldn't grasp my idea.

T: I could tell that you prepared very conscientiously for your presentation. However, some of your language was hard to understand because the stress was not correct.

S: What do you mean by "stress"?

T: Stress means emphasizing certain sounds. It is important to help clarify your meaning and make your speech sound more natural. If you don't use stress, or put the stress in the wrong place, it can cause problems with understanding.

S: I see. Could you give me some examples from my presentation?

T: For example, when you were saying the words "**pho**tograph", "pho**to**grapher" or "photo**gra**phic", the stress is in a different place in each word. You mixed the stresses up, which made it harder to follow you.

S: Are there any rules about where to put the stress in words?

T: There are some "rules of thumb", but for more complicated words or the key vocabulary in your presentation, it is better to look at the phonetic spelling in a dictionary. You will find a symbol like an apostrophe before the stressed syllable, for example, /fə 'tɒ grə fə/.

S: That's helpful to know. I also noticed that when native speakers talk, they stress some sounds in a sentence more than other sounds. Should I also pay attention to this?

T: Absolutely! Spoken English has a rhythmic stress pattern. Just as some sounds in words are stressed more than others, some sounds in sentences also have more stress. Mastering this can help your spoken English become more natural and fluent.

S: But how do I know which of the sounds to stress? It seems so complicated.

T: It can appear a bit difficult, but in English, the function of stress is just to help emphasize meaning or your feelings about what you are saying. For example, just now you naturally stressed the word "complicated".

S: Yes, I did that without thinking. Does this mean that the stress is normally placed on the most important words in a sentence?

T: Sure. A good way to think about it is to imagine you are in a noisy room and think about what words you would emphasize to make sure someone can get your message, even if they aren't able to hear every word.

S: Thank you. That is helpful. Is there any good way to practice before my next presentation?

T: I would recommend that you find some TV programs, podcasts, or recorded lectures, listen to them, and copy the stress patterns used by the presenters. In this way, the ideas we have talked about will eventually become second nature, and you will find it much easier next time.

Supplementary Materials

1. A speech—"Learning a Language Will Change Your Life for Good"
2. A lecture—"Language Acquisition"
3. A speech—"The Secrets of Learning a New Language"

Unit 6

Language History

1. "The history of a language is the history of its speakers and their culture."

—Bill Bryson (1951–), American-British journalist and author

2. "Language is the blood of the soul into which thoughts run and out of which they grow."

—Oliver Wendell Holmes (1809–1894), American author, poet, physician, and polymath

Lead-in

Human language is one of the most complex and fascinating aspects of our species. It allows us to communicate ideas, thoughts, and emotions to each other and has been a crucial factor in our evolution and development. The history of language dates back to the beginning of human civilization and has undergone various changes over time. What distinguishes human communication from that of animals? How does language change? Is it important to preserve the variety of human languages? Please review the expressions from the Preparing to Speak box and use them in discussion with your classmates.

Preparing to Speak

Match the words and phrase with their definitions.

1. abstract
2. clue
3. dialect
4. evolve
5. extinct
6. gestural language
7. great ape
8. modify
9. verbal
10. vocal

a. no longer existing or living
b. a type of communication relying on hand signals, facial expressions, and other nonverbal cues
c. involving the use of spoken or written words
d. involving the use of the voice, including speech and singing
e. a piece of information that helps solve a problem or mystery
f. conceptual or theoretical, rather than concrete or physical
g. to change and develop gradually in organisms over time
h. a language used only in a particular area or by a particular group
i. an animal from the group of animals that includes gorillas, orang-utangs, and chimpanzees
j. to change something slightly, usually to improve it or make it more acceptable

Unit 6
Language History

Learning Objectives

This unit will lead you to explore the origin of human language and its evolution into the complex communication system that we use today, and in particular the evolution of English from its humble beginning as a Germanic dialect to its position as a global language. Upon completion of this unit, you will be able to

√ know the general history of the human language and the English language;

√ understand the use of abstract terms and concepts in a speech;

√ identify various kinds of accent in spoken English;

√ apply techniques in speech delivery.

Listening Focus

Terms & Concepts

In academic contexts, terms or concepts are frequently employed to discuss intangible or complex ideas. While these enrich the depth of understanding, they can also be abstract and technical, presenting challenges for listeners. To mitigate these obstacles, several techniques are commonly utilized to aid the audience in understanding them more effectively.

- **Defining terms:** Listen for clear definitions of abstract terms. Speakers may introduce a term and then explain its meaning or significance. Look out for phrases such as "this term refers to", "by definition", or "what we mean by...".

- **Explaining concepts:** Pay attention when speakers describe what these terms or concepts involve and how they function within a particular context. They might break down complex ideas into simpler parts or explain a step-by-step process.

- **Providing examples:** Notice when speakers illustrate abstract concepts with relevant examples. These examples make the concepts more tangible and demonstrate their application in real-life scenarios. Listen for phrases such as "for instance", "such as", or "to illustrate".

- **Drawing comparisons:** Identify moments when speakers relate new concepts to familiar ones. Comparing abstract ideas to everyday experiences or well-known concepts helps listeners grasp their meaning more easily. Look for phrases such as "similar to", "like", or "analogous to".

Additionally, strategies such as understanding the context in which these concepts are discussed and connecting abstract concepts to real-life situations can significantly enhance comprehension. By actively listening for these cues, the audience can overcome the obstacles to understanding abstract terms or concepts presented in academic speeches and discussions in English.

Section A

Introduction to the listening material: The short video presentation from TED-Ed briefly introduces how language evolved from gestural communication to gestural language and then to the spoken language, which in turn, eventually led to the dominance of the human species on the planet.

Glossary

Study the words and phrases in the glossary, especially the unfamiliar ones. Do you know how to pronounce or use them in sentences? Use a dictionary to find out more information if necessary.

Words

abstraction	*n.*	the quality of being abstract 抽象
articulate	*adj.*	clearly expressed or pronounced 发音清晰的
bipedalism	*n.*	the condition of being two-footed or of using two feet for motion 二足性
bonobo	*n.*	a chimpanzee with black face and black hair, found in the forest of the Congo River basin 倭黑猩猩
chimp	*n.*	informal term for chimpanzee 黑猩猩
controversy	*n.*	an argument, especially a public one, between sides holding opposing views （公开的）争论

Unit 6
Language History

dominance	*n.*	power or influence over others 优势；支配地位
envisage	*v.*	to imagine what will happen in the future 想象；展望
exploit	*n.*	a brave, exciting, or interesting act 不凡之举
genus	*n.*	a group into which animals, plants, etc. that have similar characteristics are divided, smaller than a family and larger than a species（动植物的）属
homo	*n.*	a group of primates that includes early and modern humans 人属，人类
ignite	*v.*	to arouse the passions of; to excite 点燃，激发
intimate	*adj.*	having a close and friendly relationship 亲密的；密切的
lineage	*n.*	the series of families that someone comes from originally 世系；家系；血统
motor	*adj.*	connected with movement of the body that is produced by muscles; connected with the nerves that control movement 肌肉运动的；运动神经的
open-ended	*adj.*	without any limits, aims or dates fixed in advance 无限制的；开放式的
pantomime	*v.*	to communicate by means of gesture and facial expression 打手势
perception	*n.*	the way you notice things, especially with the senses 知觉；感知
Pleistocene	*n.*	the geologic time from about 2.6 million to 12,000 years ago characterized by the appearance and worldwide spread of hominins, and the extinction of numerous land mammals 更新世
predator	*n.*	an animal that kills and eats other animals 捕食者
scenario	*n.*	a description of how things might happen in the future 设想；方案
sequence	*n.*	the order that events, actions, etc. happen in or should happen in 顺序，次序
triple	*v.*	to become or to make something three times as much or as many 增长三倍；使增至三倍

unprecedented	*adj.*	that has never happened, been done, or been known before 前所未有的
untangle	*v.*	to make something that is complicated or confusing easier to deal with or understand 整理；厘清
vocalize	*v.*	to say or sing sounds or words 发声；说（话）；唱（歌）

Phrases

correspond to	to match 符合……
homo sapien	modern humans considered together as a species 智人；现代人
motor function	an umbrella term used to describe any activity or movement which is completed due to the use of motor neurons 运动机能
vocal tract	the airway used in the production of speech, especially the passage above the larynx, including the pharynx, mouth, and nasal cavities 声道，声腔

Task 1 Analytical Listening

Watch the video for the first time and complete the summary of the speech.

Language, Evolution's Great Mystery

The story of a bonobo using abstract symbols to communicate with humans leads to the question: What is language?

Human language is different from other animals' calls and gestures in that it can be used to (1) _____ and to (2) _____. Moreover, any child can learn any of the 7,000 distinct languages, which indicates there is (3) _____ underlying all human languages.

Though great apes give a potential clue to the origins of language, the exact time of language emergence is still unclear due to (4) _____ of many ape species. It is believed that language may have begun to take shape (5) _____ years ago, when (6) _____ tripled and (7) _____ freed the hands for communication. Meanwhile, there was the

Unit 6
Language History

transition from gestural communication to (8) _____ and then to spoken language which depends on (9) _____. The emergence of speech may have led to (10) _____ of human species.

Task 2 Detailed Listening

1. Watch the video clips and fill in the blanks with appropriate terms, concepts or their definitions, examples, and explanations.

Terms or Concepts	Definitions, Examples, or Explanations
The bonobo developed unprecedented communication ability.	It communicates not through gestures, but using (1) _____ _____ to create sequences to make requests, answer verbal questions, and refer to (2) _____.
(3) _____	It is about sharing stories, ideas and other abstract things in our mind.
It is fundamentally (4) _____.	It can be used to say an unlimited number of things.
(5) _____	Pointing to objects and pantomiming actions
Gestural language	(6) _____

2. Watch the video again and choose the best answer from the four choices marked A), B), C) and D).

1) The calls and gestures other species use to communicate are not language because _____.
   A) they generally correspond to specific messages that cannot be combined into complex ideas
   B) they are not distinctive or regular enough for practical communication
   C) they are created randomly and so changeable that they cannot be used for efficient communication
   D) they are a combination of sounds and gestures which are not typical features of language

2) Which of the following gave rise to our own species 2 to 3 million years ago?
   A) The chimp.　　　　　　　　B) The bonobo.
   C) The genus Homo.　　　　　D) The great ape.

3) Which of the following is the most advanced stage in language development?
   A) Abstract signing.
   B) Spoken language.
   C) Gestural language.
   D) Gestural communication.

4) Which of the following is correct?
   A) Great apes gesture to each other in the wild equally as freely as they vocalize.
   B) The lineage that links the great apes to humans can be traced back continuously for more than 4 million years ago.
   C) Our closest ancestors, the Neanderthals and Denisovans, were capable of articulate speech.
   D) Gestural language can be free from the help of visuals in communication.

5) Our species probably started to dominate the Earth because _____.
   A) spoken words freed human hands from making gestures for other important activities
   B) language emerged later, which is more complex than other animals' calls and gestures
   C) human beings can not only use spoken language but also gestural language
   D) human beings are bipedal which enables them to use both their hands and mouths for more efficient communication

Task 3 Critical Listening

Watch the video for the third time and discuss the following questions with your language partner.

1) What does language mean for humanity? Explain this based on your understanding of the content of the video talk and your point of view.

2) Deaf and dumb people use sign language. What are the disadvantages of sign language compared with normal language? Are there any differences between the gestures that animals use for communication and human sign language?

Section B

Introduction to the listening material: This video presentation from ClickView introduces the idea that English originates from the dialects spoken by some Germanic tribes in the 5th century, and was later enriched by words from the languages of invaders. Thereafter, more English words were created with the technological changes. Although English is now the universal language in the world with a rich and complex vocabulary, it can still trace its origins back to the Old English of the Anglo Saxons.

Glossary

Study the words and phrases in the glossary, especially the unfamiliar ones. Do you know how to pronounce or use them in sentences? Use a dictionary to find out more information if necessary.

Words

astrology	*n.*	the study of the positions of the stars and the movements of the planets in the belief that they influence human affairs 占星术
carpenter	*n.*	a person whose job is making and repairing wooden objects and structures 木匠
Celtic	*n.*	a branch of the Indo-European family of languages 凯尔特语
Christianity	*n.*	a religion based on the life and teachings of Jesus 基督教
complexion	*n.*	the natural color, texture, and appearance of the skin, especially of the face 面色
devastating	*adj.*	causing a lot of harm or damage 毁灭性的
dominion	*n.*	an area that is ruled by one person or government 领土
dwell	*v.*	to live as a resident; to reside 居住
gadget	*n.*	a small specialized mechanical or electronic device 小器具
gallows	*n.*	a wooden frame used for killing criminals by hanging 绞刑架
Germanic	*adj.*	relating to Germany or its people, language, or culture 日耳曼语族的
gloat	*v.*	to feel or express great, often malicious, pleasure or self-satisfaction 幸灾乐祸

illustrate	*v.*	to clarify or explain, as by the use of examples or comparisons 阐明
jargon	*n.*	the specialized language of a trade, profession, or similar group 行话
keen	*v.*	to lament the dead 恸哭
lodge	*v.*	to live in a place temporarily 寄住
missionary	*n.*	a person sent by a church into an area to carry on religious or humanitarian work 传教士
rage	*v.*	to move or surge with great violence 激烈进行
ransack	*v.*	to go through (a place) stealing valuables and causing disarray 洗劫
raven	*n.*	a large bird with shiny black feathers 乌鸦
refined	*adj.*	having or showing well-bred feeling or taste 文雅的
rift	*n.*	a break in friendly relations 不和，分歧
runic	*adj.*	relating to alphabets of ancient Northern Europeans 古代北欧文字的
slump	*n.*	a sudden falling off or decline 突然下跌；不景气
sonnet	*n.*	a 14-line verse form often in iambic pentameter 十四行诗
subtlety	*n.*	the quality of being complicated, delicate 微妙之处
synonymous	*adj.*	having the same meaning or almost the same meaning 同义的
temperate	*adj.*	moderate in degree or quality 温和的
thee	*pron.*	the objective case of you (thou) [古] 你（宾格）
thou	*pron.*	the nominative case of you [古] 你（主格）
thine	*pron.*	of, belonging to, or associated in some way with you (thou) [古] 你的
thrive	*v.*	to grow vigorously; to flourish 繁荣兴旺
undergo	*v.*	to experience or be subjected to 经历
untrimmed	*adj.*	not having been made tidier or more level 未修饰的

Unit 6
Language History

upheaval	*n.*	a strong, sudden, or violent disturbance, as in politics, social conditions, etc. 剧变
vulgar	*adj.*	deficient in taste, consideration, or refinement 庸俗不雅的
warmonger	*n.*	a person who advocates or attempts to stir up a war 好战分子

Phrases

die out	to become weaker or less common and then disappear completely 灭绝，消失
in full swing	at the most effective or highest level of operation or activity 活跃；蓬勃高涨

Task 1 Analytical Listening

Watch the video for the first time and complete the outline of it.

The History of English

Main Points	Supporting Details
(1) _____ origin of English	The tribes of Angles, Saxons, and Jutes from modern-day (2) _____ invaded Britain in the (3) _____. Their different dialects evolved into Old English.
Norse and Danish origin of English	The Vikings, Danes, and Norsemen invaded Britain in (4) _____ and introduced thousands of new words into Old English.
The poem of (5) _____	It is the oldest known poem written in Old English. The poem is about the (6) _____ of an old man who lost his son.

(Continued)

Main Points	Supporting Details
French influence	The (7) _____ conquered England in 1066 and their language became the language of court, business, and the ruling classes. Many French words entered English and (8) _____ of some words in English were changed.
Latin influence	In 597, words of Latin origin were brought to England by (9) _____ as he introduced Christianity. Later, more Latin words entered English to meet the need of innovation and advances in science and art during (10) _____ in the 16th century.
Standardization of the language	With the invention of (11) _____ in the 15th century there was a great need for standardization in words, spelling, and grammar of English.
Shakespeare's influence	As a master of English, Shakespeare invented more than (12) _____ words by changing nouns into verbs, adding prefixes or suffixes, etc.
The influence of the Industrial Revolution	It was an age of (13) _____, which created the need for new words to describe life and economy.
(14) _____	English is now (15) _____ for business, entertainment, tourism, technology, international communications, and trade. It has the largest vocabulary of any language which is incredibly rich and complex. The author of *Life of Pi*, remarked, "English is the language in which I best express the subtlety of life."

Task 2 Detailed Listening

1. Watch the video clips and fill in the blanks with appropriate terms and concepts, or their definitions, examples, or explanations.

1) _____ are people who come from a region called Engle and their language is where the word "English" originates.

2) _____ tell of heroic journeys and bloody battles.

3) Old English developed into Middle English as some of its rules were changed and words from other languages, especially _____, joined in.

4) _____ refers to the distinct change in vowel pronunciation in the Renaissance period when English vowels _____.

5) _____ is a shared language used by speakers whose native languages are different, such as English which is widely used in communication in the world today.

2. Watch the video again and complete the following sentences with appropriate details.

1) Germanic tribes invaded Britain in the 5th century and drove away the _____ into modern-day Wales, Scotland, and Ireland.

2) Many of the words of Latin origin brought to Anglo Saxon by Saint Augustine in 597 relate to _____; others refer to aspects of daily life.

3) It is relatively easy for words from the language of the old Norse to be integrated into English because it has _____.

4) The poem *Beowulf* was written in Old English using a version of the _____ alphabet.

5) The English alphabet we use today derives from the Latin alphabet which was first introduced into England by _____ around the 7th century.

6) In the late 900s King _____ used the English language to try to build a unified national identity amongst Britons.

7) When the Normans ruled England, the French language was considered _____ than the vulgar English tongue.

8) During the Hundred Years War _____ became the first king with _____ as his native language since the Norman Conquest.

9) During the Industrial Revolution in the 19th century, new words like "boom", "bust", "slump", and "depression" were used to describe the states of _____.

10) In American English "_____" is used instead of "rubbish", "_____" is used for the season rather than "autumn".

Task 3 Critical Listening

Watch the video for the third time and discuss the following questions with your language partner.

1) English is the result of a long evolution and therefore contains words of various origins including Germanic, French, Greek, Latin, etc. What are the advantages of a language with this feature?

2) English is now the lingua franca of the 21st century. What influence may such a universal language have on us?

Speech Workshop

Delivering a Speech

A speech is much more than words. It involves tone, pace, gesture, and eye contact. A successful speech is a performance that shows enthusiasm, sincerity, and commitment. Crucially, the passion for the topic should shine through above all else for the audience to perceive. This can be conveyed through facial expressions, vocal variation, and emphatic delivery.

This unit will delve into several speaking techniques aimed at maximizing the impact of speeches. Topics covered will include setting up an optimal speech environment, employing body language and vocal dynamics to convey emotions effectively, and selecting an appropriate delivery style to ensure the message is both expressive and meaningful.

Preparation of the Environment

To ensure a smooth presentation and minimize distractions, it is important to arrange the environment appropriately. Begin by checking the operation of the audiovisual equipment and preparing a backup plan in case of any malfunctions. Turn off any unused equipment and remove unnecessary information from the boards. Adjust the windows to optimize audience visibility, auditory clarity, and overall comfort. Ensure the lighting is sufficient to clearly illuminate the speaker, particularly their eyes and facial expressions. Finally, systematically organize all notes and materials prior to starting the presentation.

Body Language

Firstly, dress appropriately for the occasion and maintain a tidy appearance. This projects a positive and professional image to the audience. It significantly impacts their perception of competence, credibility, and confidence.

When walking to the front of the room, carry yourself confidently, knowing there are interesting and engaging materials to share with the audience. Stand tall on the stage with a balanced weight, and step out from behind the podium during the speech, allowing the audience to see you as an open and accessible speaker, not just a face behind a podium.

Typically, start and end the speech in the center of the stage. During the speech, move right or left, or step closer to the audience in a large room to maintain engagement. This movement can help ease nerves. Use hand gestures, head movements, and eye contact to make the speech more compelling and trustworthy, helping the listeners connect better. For instance, use fingers for listing points, stretch out arms to indicate something grand, or use pointing gestures to emphasize importance. However, be cautious not to overuse gestures or move aimlessly, as this can distract the audience.

Vocal Variation

Vocal variations in speed, force, and intonation can enhance communication and maintain audience attention. These variations occur naturally in daily conversations with friends and family, and our speeches can benefit similarly.

Speaking to an audience generally requires a slower pace than normal conversation, as it takes the audience more time to hear and understand the message than it takes for the speaker to articulate it. Slower speaking helps increase perceived gravitas and allows the audience to digest complex information more easily.

The speaker might speed up to convey excitement or urgency and slow down to emphasize importance, sadness, or confusion. The combination of slow, fast, and medium speed makes a speech more engaging.

To ensure everyone can hear comfortably, minimize noise distractions in the room and avoid talking over laughter or applause. In large venues, using a microphone is advisable. Checking for positive feedback from people in the back ensures the speech is being heard well and shows the speaker cares about the audience's experience. Emphasize key points by speaking louder and naturally drop the volume when sharing a sad story. Typically, start a speech loud to grab attention and finish loud to create a rousing and impressive ending.

In addition to volume changes, varying intonation is crucial. For example, rising intonation expresses uncertainty or doubt, while falling intonation is used for declarative statements, showing confidence and control.

These vocal skills help avoid a monotonous speech that sounds boring and emotionless. To improve vocal variations and delivery, practice with tongue twisters, raps, and funny voices. These exercises help transition to a natural variation in speed, volume, and intonation.

Primary Types of Delivery

Before practicing a speech, it's crucial to choose a specific type of delivery. There are four primary types: speaking with a script, speaking with notes, speaking from memory, and impromptu speaking. The choice depends on the type of information, preparation time, and the speaker's ability.

If precision and careful wording are essential, such as in news reporting or official statements, using a script or memorizing the speech may be appropriate. However, reading from a script can sound stiff and detract from energy and spontaneity. Memorizing requires ample preparation but can result in a polished delivery.

Impromptu speaking demands quick thinking, confidence, broad knowledge, and effective communication. It is typically used for short speeches like event welcomes, toasts, or expressions of gratitude.

Considering the pros and cons, many speakers consider speaking from notes as the ideal method of delivery that strikes a balance between them. Using notes allows the speaker to maintain eye contact with the audience while guiding the speech. This approach keeps the delivery natural and engages the audience without the burden of memorization.

To effectively utilize vocal variation, body language, and the chosen delivery method, adequate practice and rehearsal are essential. This preparation ensures the speech is delivered within the allotted time, boosts the speaker's confidence, and minimizes anxiety during the performance.

Task 1   Pair Work: Listen and Share

Watch the video presentation of "The History of English", and take notes about the body language and vocal aspects of the speaker. Then exchange with your language partner the information you have collected and improve your notes.

Task 2 Unit Project

Compose a 3-minute speech on the topic of language history. Practice delivering it with the help of the techniques and tips you have learned in this unit. You will present the speech in your group and help each other improve speech delivery.

Pronunciation Workshop

Accent Variation

English is widely recognized as a global language, with approximately 1.5 billion speakers worldwide. However, the way English is spoken varies greatly across different regions and cultures, resulting in numerous distinct accents. These accents are influenced by a variety of factors, including geography, history, social class, education, ethnicity, and technology.

One of the most prominent English accents is British English, spoken in the United Kingdom, Ireland, and Commonwealth countries. British English has several variations, such as **Received Pronunciation (RP)** and Estuary English, which reflect social and regional differences. RP is commonly associated with the upper class and formal settings, whereas Estuary English is more informal and associated with the southeastern region of England.

In contrast, American English is the dominant variant in the United States and Canada, with several sub-varieties, such as **General American (GA)** English and Southern American English. GA is often considered the standard or neutral accent in the United States, whereas Southern American English is associated with the southern region's culture and history.

Other English-speaking countries and regions, such as Australia, New Zealand, South Africa, and the Caribbean, also have distinct accents.

Furthermore, English accents can be influenced by non-native speakers of English around the world. In countries where English is a second language, such as India, Pakistan, and Nigeria, the English carries distinctive local features resulting from the influence of local languages, culture, and educational systems.

Of all the English accents, RP and GA are two of the most common accents in the world now. For English learners, it is essential to recognize the differences between these two accents to avoid possible misunderstandings with their speakers.

The most evident difference between the two accents is the intonation, stress, rhythm, and pronunciation of certain words. American English has a more forward and open mouth, while British English tends to be more focused on the tongue and lips. Below are some of the specific differences:

- **Intonation:** RP speakers tend to have a more varied and musical intonation pattern, while GA speakers have a more even intonation pattern.

- **Stress:** RP has a more evident difference in stress between syllables, while GA stresses syllables less, with a subtler difference between stressed and unstressed syllables.

- **Rhythm:** In British English, there are often slight pauses between words, while in American English, syllables in a sentence are more evenly spaced.

- **Vowel sounds:** RP has more exaggerated, rounded, and higher-pitched vowel sounds, while GA tends to have flatter vowel sounds. For instance, in RP the word "class" is pronounced as /ɑː/, while in GA, it is pronounced as /æ/. /ɔ/ as in "hot" and /ɔ/ as in "pot" are both pronounced as /ɑː/ in GA.

- **Rhoticity:** One of the most noticeable differences is that GA is generally rhotic, while RP is not. This means that in GA, an "r" sound is usually pronounced whenever it appears in a word, such as in the words "park" and "word". In RP, it is only pronounced when immediately followed by a vowel sound, such as in the words "risk", "run" and "error".

- RP speakers also pronounce the voiceless stops /t/, /d/, and /k/ sounds more forcefully with a stronger aspiration, while GA speakers tend to use a subtler pronunciation.

In general, GA speakers sound more relaxed and casual, while RP speakers sound more formal and educated. However, both accents are widely used and accepted across the English-speaking world.

Task 1 Listen and Identify: Accent Variation

Listen to the following conversation between two students provided by Adam Rose, an English lecturer at Tsinghua University. The first speaker is a senior student speaking in GA and the second student speaks in RP. Try to find some examples from the conversation to illustrate their accent differences.

A British student has recently arrived at a U.S. university for study. He is interviewed by a senior student from his department.

American Student: Hi, I'm a senior in the math department here. We are doing interviews with some of the freshmen to see how they are adapting to college life. Can I ask you some questions?

British Student: Yes, I am a first year. Please ask away.

American Student: Wow, that is a great accent. Are you Australian?

British Student: No, I'm from Britain—don't worry though it's an easy mistake to make.

American Student: So sorry! It was hard for me to know where you are from.

British Student: It's fine. We have a lot of different accents in the U.K., so it can be a bit tricky even for us.

American Student: So, how have your first few weeks been? How does it compare to back home?

British Student: It's been fantastic. The university, sorry, college, is huge, and the maths, sorry, "math", department has some great professors.

American Student: How about the people? How do Americans compare to Brits?

British Student: Everybody has been so friendly! In Britain, some people are cautious about speaking to strangers, but here people are so helpful.

American Student: That's awesome! Have you had any problems with adjusting to the culture?

British Student: Not so much, but I have had some problems with the language.

American Student: But we both speak English! And I know you guys watch lots of American movies and TV shows, surely the language must be one of the easier things about moving here.

British Student: That's true. We watch lots of American films and TV programs in the U.K., so I wasn't expecting too many issues, but I have had a few major breakdowns in communication.

American Student: Can you give me an example?

British Student: One of my most embarrassing things was when I first arrived and was told to find my teacher on the first floor. I spent twenty minutes looking for the office before I realized that the first floor in America is what we call the ground floor!

American Student: How about in everyday life? I've heard that you guys call an eggplant something strange.

British Student: Yes, we call it an "aubergine", and as soon as I say tomahto, rather than tomayto, people know I am British. Many other common things have different names. For example, in Britain, I would walk along the pavement before taking a lift up to my flat whereas in America, I walk along the sidewalk before taking an elevator to my apartment.

American Student: That does sound a bit confusing. I didn't realize there were so many differences between British and American English.

British Student: Someone once said that Britain and America are two countries divided by a common language. Although I don't think it is quite that bad, I do feel like I need a dictionary sometimes.

Task 2 Make a Conversation

Write a short conversation of about 2 minutes and perform it with your language partner. One plays the role of RP speaker and the other plays that of GA speaker.

Supplementary Materials

1. A talk—"Homo Erectus and the Invention of Human Language"

2. A lecture—"The Evolution of Language: From Speech to Culture"

3. A documentary—"The Adventure of English, Episode 1: Birth of a Language"

Unit 7

Teamwork

1. *"One fence has three stakes; one hero has three helpers."*

   —Chinese proverb

2. *"Talent wins games, but teamwork and intelligence win championships."*

   —Michael Jordan (1963–), American basketball player

Lead-in

Teamwork is of paramount importance in college, as it fosters collaboration, enhances problem-solving skills, and promotes a holistic learning experience. Through teamwork, students learn how to communicate effectively, delegate tasks, and leverage each other's strengths. Additionally, working in teams exposes individuals to different viewpoints, challenging them to think critically and consider alternative solutions. Can you share a memorable experience where teamwork played a crucial role in a college project or assignment? How can you build a successful and effective team? What strategies or methods have you found effective in overcoming challenges or conflicts within a college team? How did these experiences contribute to your personal growth? Please review the expressions from the Preparing to Speak box and use them in discussion with your classmates.

Preparing to Speak

Match the words and phrase with their definitions.

1.	coordinate	a. to utilize and maximize one's unique skills, talents, and abilities to achieve success and make valuable contributions
2.	delegate	b. depending on each other
3.	leverage one's strength	c. to give a particular job, duty, right, etc. to someone else so that he or she does it for you
4.	alternative	d. to make many different things work effectively as a whole
5.	interdependent	e. the one that you can use if you do not want to use another one
6.	inadvertent	f. an exceptional or outstanding achievement in a particular area of activity
7.	miracle	g. the ability to learn, understand, and make judgments or have opinions that are based on reason
8.	indispensable	h. not intentional
9.	intelligence	i. to indicate a relationship between facts, numbers, etc. where a change in one may produce a change in the other
10.	correlate	j. absolutely necessary or vital

Unit 7
Teamwork

Learning Objectives

This unit will help you to work out the essentials of teamwork. Upon completion of this unit, you will be able to

√ apply expressions related to teamwork in discussing academic studies;

√ listen for comparison and contrast in narrations;

√ understand and apply the contraction rules of auxiliary and modal verbs in pronunciation;

√ discuss a topic related to teamwork within a group, paying attention to taking turns in the discussion.

Listening Focus

Comparison & Contrast

In a lecture, you should either recognize how the entire listening passage is organized or how different portions of the passage are related to one another. Listening skills related to comparison and contrast are essential for understanding and analyzing information presented in this manner.

To effectively utilize these skills, individuals must focus on the context of the discussion and anticipate comparison and contrast being made. By paying attention to cues such as specific words or phrases indicating similarities or differences, you can identify key ideas and distinguish between them. Taking organized notes helps you capture the main points being compared and contrasted, while actively seeking supporting details deepens comprehension. To improve your listening skills for comparison and contrast, follow these instructions below:

- **Focus on the context:** Understanding the topic or subject being discussed will help you anticipate and identify points of comparison and contrast.

- **Pay attention to cues:** Listen for words and phrases that indicate comparison or contrast is being made. Commonly used words and phrases are listed below. You may add more to the list.

For comparison	For contrast
Similarly,	In contrast,
Likewise,	By contrast,

In the same way,	On the other hand,
…is similar to that…	…differs from that…
…is comparable to that…	…contrasts with that…
…is comparable in complexity to…	…is different from…

- **Identify key ideas:** Listen for the main points or arguments being presented. Take notes of the similarities and differences between the ideas.
- **Take organized notes:** Use a structured format such as a Venn diagram, T-chart, or bullet points to jot down the main points being compared and contrasted. See Figure 7.1 and Figure 7.2 for examples of Venn diagram and T-chart.

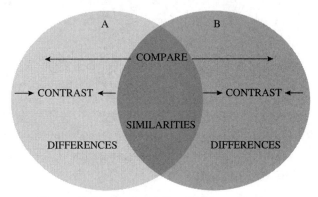

Figure 7.1　An example of a Venn diagram

Figure 7.2　An example of a T-chart

- **Practice regularly:** Continuously expose yourself to listening opportunities that involve comparison and contrast, whether through lectures, podcasts, or conversations. Regular practice will strengthen your skills over time.

Listening Practice

Section A

Introduction to the listening material: This listening material is from *The Economist*. It uses the Beatles, a legendary English rock band, as an example to illustrate what makes a team. Consisting of four members—John Lennon, Paul McCartney, George Harrison, and Ringo Starr—the Beatles became one of the most influential and commercially successful groups in the history of popular music.

Glossary

Study the words and phrases in the glossary, especially the unfamiliar ones. Do you know how to pronounce or use them in sentences? Use a dictionary to find out more information if necessary.

Words

beatifically	*adv.*	in a way that appears happy and calm, especially in a holy way 极乐地；天使般地
bewilder	*v.*	to confuse someone 使迷惑，使糊涂；难住
chart	*v.*	to arrange a plan of action 制订（行动计划）
cohesive	*adj.*	united and working together effectively 有凝聚力的；团结的
ethos	*n.*	the set of beliefs, ideas, etc. about the social behavior and relationships of a person or group（个人或团体的）精神特质，价值观，信条
ghastly	*adj.*	unpleasant and shocking 可怕的；令人震惊的
dispensable	*adj.*	more than you need and therefore not necessary; something that can be got rid of 可有可无的，非必需的

listlessly	*adv.*	in a way that shows you have no energy and enthusiasm and are unwilling to do anything needing effort 懈怠地，懒散地，无精打采地
magpie	*n.*	someone who likes to collect many different types of objects, or use many different styles 收集各式物品的人；有多种不同风格的人
reinforce	*v.*	If something reinforces an idea or opinion, it provides more proof or support for it and makes it seem true. 强化，加深，进一步证实（观点、看法等）
sheer	*adj.*	used to emphasize how very great, important, or powerful a quality or feeling is; nothing except 完全的，彻底的
snugly	*adv.*	in a way that fits closely 紧贴地；贴身地
staleness	*n.*	the quality of being boring because of being too familiar 老套，无新意
strum	*v.*	to move your fingers across the strings of a guitar or similar instrument 弹奏，拨弄（吉他或类似乐器）
thrillingly	*adv.*	in an extremely exciting way 惊心动魄地

Phrases

a staple of	a main product or part of something 主要产品；某物的主要部分
derive...from...	to get something from something else 从……中得到，从……中获得
esprit de corps	the feelings, such as being proud and loyal, shared by members of a group of people 团队精神，集体精神；集体荣誉感
keep...at bay	to prevent someone or something unpleasant from harming you 阻止，遏制（令人不快的事物）
yearn for	to wish very strongly, especially for something that you cannot have or that is very difficult to have 渴望，切盼，渴求

Unit 7 Teamwork

Task 1 Analytical Listening

Listen to the audio for the first time and complete the outline.

What Makes a Team?

Lead-in	Describing a scene in the Beatles documentary named (1) _____
Body (Three principles)	– Principle 1: Psychological (2) _____ matters to how teams come together. – Principle 2: Look here, there and everywhere for (3) _____. – Principle 3: When and how to (4) _____.
Conclusion	The highest-performing teams derive the greatest satisfaction not from each other, but from the (5) _____ they do together.

Task 2 Detailed Listening

Listen to the audio clips and fill in the blanks with the exact words or phrases you hear.

1) The question of what makes a team sing is a _____ of management research, and the Beatles documentary is a rare chance to watch a truly world-class team at work.

2) The performance of groups is not _____ with their members' average intelligence, but with characteristics such as _____ and how good teams are at giving everyone time to speak.

3) Among other things, the consultancy identified the importance of _____, the habit of keeping staleness at bay by taking risks, by learning from others, and by innovating.

4) When they first meet up, on the second day of 1969, the band has a task that fits these criteria _____: To write an album's worth of new songs in just a matter of days and perform them on a TV special.

5) Although technical ability is not the only determinant of success, sheer _____ helped.

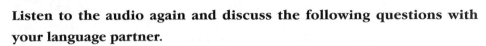

Task 3 Critical Listening

Listen to the audio again and discuss the following questions with your language partner.

1) Would you like to be the "Ringo" in your team? Why or why not?

2) Reflecting on Google's Project Aristotle findings, why do you think setting specific, challenging, and attainable goals is crucial for team success? Can you provide examples or scenarios where this principle would be particularly applicable?

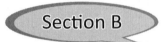

Introduction to the listening material: In this TED talk—"How to Turn a Group of Strangers into a Team?", Amy Edmondson, a business school professor introduces the concept of "teaming". Recalling stories of teamwork on the fly, such as the incredible rescue of 33 miners trapped half a mile underground in Chile in 2010, Edmondson shares the elements needed to turn a group of strangers into a quick-thinking team that can nimbly respond to challenges.

Glossary

Study the words and phrases in the glossary, especially the unfamiliar ones. Do you know how to pronounce or use them in sentences? Use a dictionary to find out more information if necessary.

Words

configuration	n.	the particular arrangement or pattern of a group of related things 布局；构造，结构
crack	v.	to find a solution to a problem 解决（问题）；破译
deliverable	n.	something that can be provided or achieved as a result of a process 可以做到的事
embody	v.	to represent a quality or an idea exactly 具体表现；体现

expertise	n.	a high level of knowledge or skill 专门技能（知识）；专长	
filth	n.	thick, unpleasant dirt 污物，污秽	
humility	n.	the quality of not being proud because you are aware of your bad qualities 谦逊，谦恭	
inadvertently	adv.	in a way that is not intentional 无意地	
persevere	v.	to try to do or continue doing something in a determined way, despite having problems 锲而不舍，坚持不懈	
quest	n.	a long search for something that is difficult to find, or an attempt to achieve something difficult 探索；寻求；追求	
refuge	n.	(a place that gives) protection or shelter from danger, trouble, unhappiness, etc. 避难（所）；庇护（所）	
scarcity	n.	a situation in which something is not easy to find or get 缺乏；不足；短缺	
silo	n.	a part of a company, organization, or system that does not communicate with, understand, or work well with other parts（公司、机构或系统内部与其他单位不联系、不合作的）孤立单位	
spawn	v.	to cause something new, or many new things, to grow or start suddenly（使）产生，（使）突然增长	
stake	n.	the risk 风险	

Phrases

aspire to	to have a strong wish or hope to do or have something 追求；渴望；有志于
be hardwired to	If someone or something is hardwired to do a particular thing, they automatically do it and find it hard to change that behavior. 本能的（指不可改变的）
from scratch	from the beginning, without using anything that already exists 从头开始，从零开始

get a glimpse of	to manage to see something for a short time 短时间看某物
pick up	to increase or improve 增加；提高；改进
see eye to eye	If two people see eye to eye, they agree with each other.（两人）意见一致

Task 1 Analytical Listening

Watch the video for the first time and complete the outline of the talk.

How to Turn a Group of Strangers into a Team?

Introduction	**A beginning story** A massive collapse has left (1) _____ trapped half a mile below some of the hardest rock in the world. This remarkable story is a case study in (2) _____.	
	Definition of teaming Teaming is teamwork (3) _____.	
Comparison & contrast between teaming and sports team	**Teaming** You can think of teaming as a kind of pickup game in the park, in contrast to (4) _____.	**Sports team** Sports team wins because (5) _____. Sports team embodies the definition of a team, (6) _____.
Importance & barriers of teaming	– Teaming is especially needed for work that's (7) _____. – Example: Smart cities A smart-city software start-up: (8) _____ is a major barrier to building the future that we aspire to build. And (9) _____ would help to overcome this problem. It's hard to team if you see others as (10) _____.	

Task 2 Detailed Listening

Watch the video again and choose the best answer from the four choices marked A), B), C) and D).

1) In the context of the TED talk, how does teaming differ from traditional sports teams?
   A) It involves practicing together over time.
   B) It requires coordination across various boundaries.
   C) It is focused on achieving a shared outcome.
   D) It relies on stable and well-practiced groups.

2) According to the TED talk, why is teaming becoming more prevalent in today's work environments?
   A) There is an increased emphasis on stable and bounded teams.
   B) The luxury of stable teams is not available for most work.
   C) Fast-paced operations require stable and well-practiced teams.
   D) Different specialties and areas of expertise necessitate stable teams.

3) According to the TED talk, what do creating an animated film and taking care of patients in the emergency room have in common?
   A) They require fixed roles and deliverables.
   B) They involve working with stable teams throughout the process.
   C) They rely on unpredictable outcomes and constantly changing configurations.
   D) They necessitate individual effort rather than collaboration.

4) Why does the speaker mention the quest for smart cities?
   A) To highlight the need for teamwork in addressing complex problems.
   B) To emphasize the importance of fixed roles and deliverables in city planning.
   C) To argue against the use of technology in designing smart cities.
   D) To illustrate the impact of climate change on urbanization trends.

5) According to the speaker, what was a major challenge encountered during the smart city project mentioned?
   A) Lack of cooperation between software engineers and architects.
   B) Difficulties in breaking ground and initiating construction.
   C) Clash of professional cultures and differences in perspectives.
   D) Inability to secure funding for the project.

6) In the Chilean mining rescue mission, what qualities or behavior contributed to the success of the teaming process?
   A) Patience and perseverance in the face of daily failures.
   B) Strict adherence to a predefined plan and timeline.

C) Limited involvement of diverse expertise and international collaboration.

D) Reliance on traditional mining techniques rather than experimentation.

7) According to the speaker, what is situational humility in the context of teaming?

A) The willingness of leaders to acknowledge their lack of expertise.

B) A sense of psychological safety that allows for risk-taking.

C) The ability to overcome professional culture clashes through curiosity.

D) The mindset of being open to learning from others and embracing new ideas.

8) What message does the speaker suggest organizations should avoid when welcoming newcomers?

A) Emphasizing the importance of competition and individual success.

B) Encouraging a scarcity mindset where only a few can succeed.

C) Fostering an environment of independent work.

D) Promoting collaboration among team members.

Task 3 Critical Listening

Watch the video for the third time and discuss the following questions with your language partner.

1) What are the potential benefits and challenges that arise from college students engaging in team projects and working with classmates with varying backgrounds, expertise, and schedules? Can you offer any examples?

2) In what ways do perceptions of scarcity and competition among college students hinder effective teaming, and how can individuals shift their mindset to view their peers as collaborators rather than competitors, thereby unlocking the potential for improved results in academic endeavors?

Speech Workshop

Turn-Taking

Turn-taking is a fundamental aspect of academic discussions that ensures effective communication and thoughtful exchange of ideas. In an academic setting, turn-taking refers to the orderly and organized process of individuals taking their respective turns to contribute to the discussion. This practice promotes equal participation, fosters active engagement, and allows for the expression of diverse viewpoints.

To facilitate smooth turn-taking, participants should be attentive to verbal and nonverbal cues indicating when someone has finished speaking or wishes to contribute. Pauses, gestures, and eye contact can signal the intention to speak, while a nod or other acknowledgment demonstrates respect for the current speaker. It is essential to exercise patience and avoid interrupting others, as this can disrupt the flow of the discussion and hinder understanding.

When it is your turn to speak, it is important to express your thoughts clearly and succinctly. Present your arguments, provide supporting evidence or examples, and engage with the ideas already expressed by others. Acknowledge and build upon previous contributions, fostering a collaborative and inclusive environment.

Here are a few useful expressions for turn-taking in academic discussions:

- May I add to that?
- I'd like to contribute my perspective.
- If I may chime in...
- Could I share my thoughts on this topic?
- Building upon what [previous speaker] mentioned...
- In relation to that point, I believe...
- I have something to offer regarding this issue.
- Allow me to provide some insights.
- I'd like to respond to [previous speaker's] comment.
- To expand on what has been said...

These expressions can be used to politely and assertively signal your intention to take a turn and contribute to the ongoing discussion. Remember to use them respectfully and considerately, ensuring that you acknowledge and build upon the ideas expressed by others.

Task 1 Pair Work: Listen and Share

Each pair picks one of the following two topics: (1) the benefits of teamwork in college; (2) the drawbacks of teamwork in college.

Student A begins the discussion and talks for 1 minute while Student B listens attentively. After Student A's turn, ask Student B to summarize the main points or ideas shared by his or her partner. Then, it's Student B's turn to contribute thoughts on the topic or answer the question while Student A actively listens. Set a specific 1-minute limit for each turn. Repeat the process, alternating turns between the students until both have had equal opportunities to speak. Encourage active listening and remind students to build upon their partner's ideas or ask follow-up questions during their turn.

Task 2 Unit Project

Run a roundtable discussion of 3–6 students on one of the following topics. Pay attention to turn-taking in your discussion.

1) Describe the benefits and challenges that arise from your experiences of working with classmates previously in college. How much do you like teamwork in comparison with individual work?

2) In many contexts, all members of a group can benefit from the efforts of each member and all can benefit substantially from collective action. However, there might be a free rider who receives benefits without any contribution to the team. What do you think about the free rider problem?

Pronunciation Workshop

Contractions of Auxiliary & Modal Verbs

Contractions are shortened forms of words created by combining two or more words. In English, contractions of auxiliary and modal verbs are commonly used in spoken language for ease and fluidity. Here are some common contractions of auxiliary verbs, modal verbs, and their pronunciations.

Auxiliary Verbs

- **be**

    I'm (I am)—pronounced /aɪm/

    you're (you are)—pronounced /jʊr/ or /jɔːr/

    he's/she's/it's (he is/she is/it is)—pronounced /hiz/, /ʃiz/, /ɪts/

    we're (we are)—pronounced /wɪr/ or /wɜːr/

    they're (they are)—pronounced /ðɛr/ or /ðeər/

- **have**

    I've (I have)—pronounced /aɪv/

    you've (you have)—pronounced /jʊv/ or /jʌv/

    he's/she's/it's (he has/she has/it has)—pronounced /hiz/, /ʃiz/, /ɪts/

    we've (we have)—pronounced /wiv/

    they've (they have)—pronounced /ðeɪv/

- **will**

    I'll (I will)—pronounced /aɪl/

    you'll (you will)—pronounced /jʊl/

    he'll/she'll/it'll (he will/she will/it will)—pronounced /hil/, /ʃil/, /ɪtl/

    we'll (we will)—pronounced /wil/

    they'll (they will)—pronounced /ðeɪl/

- **would**

    I'd (I would)—pronounced /aɪd/

    you'd (you would)—pronounced /jʊd/

    he'd/she'd/it'd (he would/she would/it would)—pronounced /hid/, /ʃid/, /ɪtəd/

    we'd (we would)—pronounced /wid/

    they'd (they would)—pronounced /ðeɪd/

- **had**

    I'd (I had)—pronounced /aɪd/

    you'd (you had)—pronounced /jʊd/

    he'd/she'd/it'd (he had/she had/it had)—pronounced /hid/, /ʃid/, /ɪtəd/

    we'd (we had)—pronounced /wid/

    they'd (they had)—pronounced /ðeɪd/

Modal Verbs

  can

  can't (cannot)—pronounced /kænt/

could

couldn't (could not)—pronounced /ˈkʊdənt/

will

won't (will not)—pronounced /woʊnt/

would

wouldn't (would not)—pronounced /ˈwʊdənt/

shall

shan't (shall not)—pronounced /ʃænt/ (less commonly used)

should

shouldn't (should not)—pronounced /ˈʃʊdənt/

must

mustn't (must not)—pronounced /ˈmʌsənt/

might

mightn't (might not)—pronounced /ˈmaɪtənt/ (less commonly used)

Task 1　Sample Analysis

Read after the recording. Pay attention to contractions in each sentence.

1) Yes, you're [you are] highlighting the time aspect.

2) It's [It is] also about reaching agreement.

3) What'd [What would] be the reasons something like this might happen?

4) There is usually someone in the group that'd [that would] suggest "doing it the way we've [we have] always done it".

5) If it ain't broke, don't fix it. ("Ain't" is informally used as a contraction for "am not", "is not", "are not", "has not", "have not", "do not", "does not", and "did not".)

6) A lack of diversity might mean there won't [will not] be different perspectives represented in the group itself.

Task 2 Listen and Identify: Contractions

1. Listen to the introduction of a lesson on how to avoid groupthink and identify the contractions that are used by the instructor.

   1) _____ (short for _____)

   2) _____ (short for _____)

   3) _____ (short for _____)

   4) _____ (short for _____)

2. Listen to the lecture about how to avoid groupthink provided by John P. Grima, an English lecturer at Tsinghua University. Pay attention to the contractions used in the lecture.

Supplementary Materials

1. A TED talk—"Build a Tower, Build a Team"

2. An interview—"Leaders Talk with Thomas Bach"

3. A Lecture—"How to Avoid Teamwork Disasters?"

Unit 8

Motivation

1. *"Internal impetus is the fundamental force driving the development of individuals and regions."*
   　　　　　—Xi Jinping (1953–), President of the People's Republic of China

2. *"The only way to do great work is to love what you do."*
   　　　　　—Steve Jobs (1955–2011), co-founder of Apple Inc.

Lead-in

Have you heard about a "self-managing" company? Those companies get rid of managers, i.e., they are not hierarchical and have no boss. Would you like to pursue a job in a "self-managing" company after graduation? In your opinion, what are some common challenges individuals face when it comes to self-management, and how can they be overcome? Please review the expressions from the Preparing to Speak box and use them in discussion with your classmates.

Preparing to Speak

Match the words and phrase with their definitions.

1. ambition
2. determination
3. resilience
4. discipline
5. on your own initiative
6. tenacity
7. self-control
8. focus
9. proactive
10. goal-oriented

a. the ability to continue trying to do something, although it is very difficult
b. the ability to control yourself or other people, even in difficult situations
c. you plan it and decide to do it yourself without anyone telling you what to do
d. a strong wish to achieve something
e. the ability to be happy, successful, etc. again after something difficult or bad has happened
f. the central point of something, especially of attention or interest
g. working hard to achieve good results in the tasks that one has been given
h. the determination to continue what you are doing
i. the ability to control your emotions and actions
j. taking action by causing change and not only reacting to change when it happens

Learning Objectives

This unit will enable you to understand the essentials of motivation in leading a team. Upon completion of this unit, you will be able to

√ apply expressions related to motivation in discussing academic studies;

Unit 8
Motivation

> √ apply the listening strategy of inferring the speaker's intention and attitude;
>
> √ understand and apply intonation rules in pronunciation;
>
> √ identity the key elements that make a successful seminar discussion and apply some useful expressions for engaging in a seminar discussion.

Listening Focus

Speaker's Intention & Attitude

Pragmatic understanding refers to the function of what is said and the speaker's attitude. "Function of what is said" questions test whether you can understand the underlying intentions of what is said. "Speakers' attitude" questions test whether you can understand a speaker's attitude or opinion that has not been directly expressed.

Listening skills that involve inferring the speaker's intention and attitude are crucial in understanding communication beyond the surface level. You should focus on both verbal and nonverbal cues, carefully observing the speaker's tone of voice, facial expressions, body language, and gestures. Context plays a vital role as well, providing valuable insights into the purpose of the communication. By attentively listening for implied meaning and considering the speaker's perspective, you can gain a deeper understanding of the speaker's underlying intention and attitude behind the words. Regular practice enables you to enhance skills in inferring the speaker's intention, decipher the true message being conveyed, and thus foster more meaningful interactions.

To improve your listening skills for inferring the speaker's intention and attitude, follow these instructions:

- **Focus on verbal and nonverbal cues:** Pay attention to both what the speaker says and how he or she says it. Notice his or her tone of voice, intonation, sentence stress, facial expressions, body language, and gestures, as these can provide valuable clues about his or her intention.

- **Consider the context:** Understand the situation in which the communication is taking place. The context can offer insights into the speaker's purpose, whether he or she is giving a presentation, having a conversation, or making a request.

- **Listen for implied meaning:** Be attentive to the words and phrases used by the speaker. Look out for subtle hints, implications, or suggestions that may indicate his or her underlying intention. Sometimes, what is left unsaid can be just as important as what is said. (Refer to Listening Focus of Unit 3)

- **Ask clarifying questions:** If you are unsure about the speaker's intention, don't hesitate to seek clarification. Ask open-ended questions that encourage the speaker to elaborate on his or her thoughts or provide additional context.

- **Practice active listening:** Engage fully in the conversation or presentation. Demonstrate your interest and understanding by maintaining eye contact, nodding, and providing appropriate verbal and nonverbal feedback. Active listening encourages the speaker to communicate more clearly, making it easier to infer his or her intention. (Refer to the video on Active Listening Skills)

- **Reflect and review:** After the conversation or presentation, take a moment to reflect on the speaker's intention. Review the key points and analyze the underlying message. Consider whether your initial inferences align with the overall context and the speaker's subsequent actions.

Listening Practice

Section A

Introduction to the listening material: This dialog is from "BBC Learning English". Neil and Georgina talk about company hierarchies and introduce a self-managing company—California tomato grower "Morning Star".

Glossary

Study the words and phrases in the glossary, especially the unfamiliar ones. Do you know how to pronounce or use them in sentences? Use a dictionary to find out more information if necessary.

Words

bureaucracy	n.	a system for controlling or managing a country, company, or organization that is operated by a large number of officials employed to follow rules carefully 官僚作风；官僚主义；官僚体制

coercion	n.	the use of force to persuade someone to do something that he or she is unwilling to do 强制，强迫；威逼；胁迫
empower	v.	to give someone official authority or the freedom to do something 给（某人）做……的权力；授权；使自主
excess	n.	an amount that is more than acceptable, expected, or reasonable 过分；过量；过度
governance	n.	the way that organizations or countries are managed at the highest level, and the systems for doing this（机构或国家最高层的）管理体系
hierarchy	n.	a system in which people or things are arranged according to their importance 等级制度
persuasion	n.	the action of persuading someone or of being persuaded 说服

Phrases

be held accountable	to accept responsibility for the consequences of your actions 为行为承担责任
leave behind	to remain at a lower level than others because you are not as quick to improve, develop or progress 落后
take full advantage (of)	to make good use of an opportunity to progress or achieve a goal 充分把握并利用机会

Task 1 Analytical Listening

Listen to the audio for the first time and complete the outline.

Self-Managing Company

| Lead-in | Introducing the concept of a "self-managing" company, which isn't (1) _____ and has no boss. |

Body	– **Principle 1:** Human beings should not use force or (2) _____ against other human beings. – **Principle 2:** People should keep the (3) _____ they make to each other. – **Concern:** Some employees may be (4) _____.
Conclusion	No matter whether employees are good self-managers or not, they are held (5) _____ for their work performance.

(Continued)

Task 2 Detailed Listening

Listen to the audio clips and fill in the blanks with the exact words or phrases you hear.

1) One of the biggest problems in _____ is the excess cost of management and bureaucracy.

2) Having no bosses sounds great, but the extra _____ can create more work and stress.

3) Although having no boss sounds good, if things go wrong, there's no one to _____ _____ but yourself.

4) Can you _____ how much the U.S. economy loses in excess bureaucracy and managerial costs every year?

5) Many employees react _____ to this working environment and take full advantage of it.

Task 3 Critical Listening

Listen to the audio again and discuss the following questions with your language partner.

1) We learn from the dialog that different workers respond to self-management in different ways. Some people take full advantage of this environment, while others take less advantage and may feel left behind. Which group do you think you will fit in? Why?

2) One of the concerns about self-managed companies is that the extra responsibility can create more work and stress. What other problems do you think there might be with this type of management?

Unit 8
Motivation

Section B

Introduction to the listening material: In this TED talk—"How Your Brain Responds to Stories—and Why They Are Crucial for Leaders?", leadership consultant Karen Eber demystifies what makes for effective storytelling and explains how anyone can harness it to create empathy and inspire action. It is revealed that the world's best leaders and visionaries earn trust not merely by presenting data, but also by telling great stories.

Glossary

Study the words and phrases in the glossary, especially the unfamiliar ones. Do you know how to pronounce or use them in sentences? Use a dictionary to find out more information if necessary.

Words

ace	*v.*	to do very well in an exam 考得很好
autistic	*adj.*	affected by or relating to the condition of autism, which affects the development of social and communication skills and can affect behavior 患自闭症的；与自闭症相关的
empathy	*n.*	the ability to share someone else's feelings or experiences by imagining what it would be like to be in that person's situation 同情；同感，共鸣
epicenter	*n.*	the point on the Earth's surface directly above an earthquake（地震）震中
floss	*v.*	to clean between your teeth using dental floss 用牙线清洁（牙缝）
lobe	*n.*	any part of an organ that seems to be separate in some way from the rest, especially one of the parts of the brain, lungs, or liver（尤指大脑、肺、肝等器官的）叶
navigate	*v.*	to direct the way that a ship, aircraft, etc. will travel, or to find a direction across, along, or over an area of water or

		land, often by using a map（常指借助地图）导航，确定……的方向
oxytocin	n.	a hormone that helps with labor (= the process of pushing out a baby) and helps women and female mammals to produce milk 催产素
paralyzing	adj.	causing a person or group to stop working or acting normally 瘫痪的
quote	n.	the price that a person or company says they will charge to do a piece of work 报价
resonate	v.	to make you think of another similar one 使产生联想；引起共鸣
thud	n.	the sound that is made when something heavy falls or hits something else 砰的一声；重击声；沉闷的声响

Phrases

be allergic to...	to have a strong dislike of something 对……极其反感的
Broca's area	a region of the brain that contains neurons involved in speech function 布洛卡区为语言的运动中枢，主要功能是编制发音程序
light up	If your face or eyes light up, or if a smile lights up your face, you suddenly look happy. 使高兴起来，（使）显出笑意
Wernicke's area	a structure of the brain that is believed to be involved in language comprehension 韦尼克区（又称威尼克区、沃尼克区），大脑听觉中枢，视觉性语言中枢，听觉性语言中枢

Task 1 Analytical Listening

Watch the video clips and infer the function of what is said in each clip.

1) Listen to the beginning stories of Maria and Walter. What's the key message conveyed by these two stories? What's the function of telling stories at the beginning of this TED talk?

2) What can be inferred from the statement that "Storytelling and data is actually not this either-or. It's an 'and'"?

3) What does neural coupling mean in view of the examples?

4) What's the speaker's attitude towards decision-making? Does the speaker think decision-making is a rational process or not?

5) What can be inferred about the relationship between storytelling and motivation?

Task 2 Detailed Listening

Watch the video and choose the best answer from the four choices marked A), B), C) and D).

1) Why did Walter Bettinger make a vow to always know the Dotties in his life?
   A) He failed an exam because he didn't know the name of the person who cleaned the room.
   B) He wanted to become a leader like Maria.
   C) He wanted to ace all his exams from that day forward.
   D) He thought it was important to remember the names of everyone he met.

2) What effect does storytelling have on the listener's perception of the speaker?
   A) It decreases empathy and trust towards the speaker.
   B) It has no impact on the listener's perception of the speaker.
   C) It releases oxytocin and increases trust in the speaker.
   D) It activates Wernicke's area and Broca's area in the listener's brain.

3) According to the speaker, what role do emotions play in decision-making?
   A) They have no impact on decision-making.
   B) They are only involved after a decision has been consciously made.
   C) They play a subconscious role in decision-making before we become aware of it.
   D) They are rationalizations that occur after decisions have been made.

4) What does the speaker suggest about the interpretation of data?
   A) Each person's interpretation of data is the same due to shared knowledge and experience.
   B) Data speaks for itself and does not require any interpretation or bias.
   C) The interpretation of data varies from person to person based on their own knowledge, experience, and bias.
   D) Data interpretation is guided by a universal standard, eliminating individual differences.

5) What are the three questions that a great story should answer?
   A) Who is involved, what is the outcome, and why should I care?
   B) What is the context, where is the conflict, and how does it end?
   C) Why should I care, where is the setting, and who is involved?
   D) What is the outcome, when does it take place, and how does it change?

6) According to the TED talk, why is it important to start with data and storytelling?
   A) It helps in creating a melody and harmony between data and storytelling.
   B) It allows the presenter to showcase his or her knowledge of various markets.
   C) It ensures the audience remains engaged during the entire presentation.
   D) It enables the company to break into new markets and remain competitive.

7) Why did Briana seek help in preparing her presentation to university leadership?
   A) She wanted to focus solely on presenting data.
   B) She needed assistance in connecting with the university officials.
   C) She was unsure about how to navigate the changes at university.
   D) She wanted to share Michelle's story with the leaders.

8) According to the TED talk, why are storytelling and data important in Briana's presentation?
   A) They help build ideas and tap into emotions.
   B) They provide a one-size-fits-all approach to communication.
   C) They ensure that all students graduate from university.
   D) They offer a million-dollar earning potential for individuals with autism.

Task 3 Critical Listening

Watch the video again and discuss the following questions with your language partner.

1) What is the topic for your next presentation in college? Drawing on the findings of this TED talk, what story are you going to share with the audience? How will the story help with your presentation?

2) What are some potential drawbacks or limitations of relying heavily on stories in presentations, and how can presenters strike a balance between storytelling and delivering factual or data-driven content?

Speech Workshop

Seminar Discussion

A seminar discussion is a valuable academic activity that promotes active learning, critical thinking, and meaningful engagement with the course material. It provides an opportunity to explore complex concepts, analyze different perspectives, and develop the ability to articulate and defend your ideas.

In a seminar discussion, participants come together in a small group setting, guided by an instructor or facilitator who encourages dialog and intellectual exchange. The purpose of such a discussion is to delve deeper into the subject matter, challenge assumptions, and foster a collaborative learning environment. It is important to actively listen to others, respect diverse viewpoints, and constructively contribute to the conversation. You should be prepared after reading and thoughtfully considering the assigned materials, which allows you to engage in informed discussions.

During a seminar discussion, you can utilize various expressions to effectively navigate turn-taking and contribute meaningfully to the conversation. Some useful expressions for engaging in a seminar discussion include:

- I'd like to begin by...
- From my understanding...
- In light of what we've learned, I propose...
- One possible interpretation could be...
- To play devil's advocate...
- Based on the evidence provided, I would argue that...
- Another perspective to consider is...
- Expanding on [previous speaker's] point...
- Could you clarify your position on...
- Building on what has been discussed, I suggest...

These expressions facilitate active participation, encourage critical analysis, and demonstrate a willingness to engage with diverse viewpoints. You should also listen attentively and respond thoughtfully to the contributions of others, using expressions such as:

- I agree/disagree with [speaker's name] because...
- Adding to that, I'd like to mention...
- I'd like to offer a counterpoint to consider...
- In my opinion, this approach overlooks...
- I see merit in both perspectives, but...
- Have we considered the implications of...?
- I'd like to further explore the connection between...
- It's worth noting that...
- Can we delve deeper into the underlying assumptions of...?
- Let's take a step back and examine the broader implications of...

It is also important to check whether the listeners have understood your talk by asking follow-up questions.

Task 1 Pair Work: Listen and Share

1) Each student shares an example on how effective self-management has improved self-motivation and productivity.

2) Discuss and summarize motivation strategies employed in the shared experience.

Task 2 Unit Project

Form a group of 5–6 students and hold a seminar on the topic of boosting motivation and mastering self-management.

This seminar aims to provide participants with practical strategies and insights to enhance motivation and develop effective self-management skills. Attendees will explore the key principles and techniques for maintaining high levels of motivation while effectively managing their time, energy, and resources. Through interactive discussions, activities, and real-life examples, participants will gain valuable tools to overcome obstacles, set meaningful goals, prioritize tasks, and maintain a healthy work-life balance.

Suggested seminar outline:

I. Introduction to Motivation and Self-Management

A. Definition and importance of motivation

B. Benefits of effective self-management

II. Understanding Motivation

A. Theories of motivation (e.g., Maslow's hierarchy of needs, self-determination theory)

B. Intrinsic and extrinsic motivation

C. Factors influencing motivation (e.g., goal setting, rewards, autonomy)

III. Enhancing Motivation

A. Setting meaningful goals

B. Overcoming challenges and setbacks

C. Building motivation through positive reinforcement

D. Fostering a growth mindset

IV. Effective Self-Management Techniques

A. Prioritization and time management strategies

B. Task delegation and effective decision-making

C. Procrastination management

D. Developing and maintaining focus and concentration

V. Overcoming Self-Management Challenges

A. Identifying common obstacles (e.g., distractions, lack of organization)

B. Strategies for overcoming procrastination and self-sabotage

C. Building resilience and managing stress

VI. Q&A Session

VII. Wrap-up and Conclusion

Pronunciation Workshop

Intonation

Intonation refers to the variation in pitch, which plays a crucial role in spoken English, conveying meaning, mood, and emphasis. Three main patterns of intonation shape the way we speak: **rising intonation, falling intonation**, and **rising-falling intonation**. Each pattern carries its own significance and is used in different contexts to express questions, statements, commands, emphasis, and more. Understanding these intonation patterns is essential for effective communication and natural-sounding speech in English. The following are the common functions of intonation used in English communication.

Expressing Emotions and Attitudes

- **Rising intonation:** Often indicates questions, surprise, or uncertainty. For example, "Really?" or "You're going?"
- **Falling intonation:** Typically signals statements, commands, or finality. For example, "I'm going home." or "Sit down."

Differentiating Sentence Types

- **Statements:** Usually end with a falling intonation. For example, "She is going to the store."
- **Yes/No questions:** Often end with a rising intonation. For example, "Are you coming?"
- **Wh- questions:** Typically end with a falling intonation. For example, "Where are you going?"
- **Tag questions:** End with a rising intonation when the speaker is genuinely asking for confirmation and end with a falling intonation when the speaker already knows the answer. For example, "You're coming, aren't you?"

Highlighting Information

- **Focus and emphasis:** Highlight the most important information in a sentence. For example, "I asked *her* to do it," versus "I asked her to do *it*."
- **Contrast:** Show contrast or correction. For example, "I wanted tea, not coffee."

Indicating Continuation or Completion

- **Continuation:** Rising intonation can indicate that the speaker has not finished his or her thought. For example, "I went to the store, and…"
- **Completion:** Falling intonation indicates the end of a thought or sentence. For example, "I went to the store."

Unit 8
Motivation

Managing Conversations

- **Turn-taking:** Intonation helps manage the flow of conversation, indicating when a speaker is finished and it's another person's turn to speak. A falling intonation often signifies the end of a turn.

- **Agreement or disagreement:** Intonation can signal agreement or disagreement. For example, a rising intonation might imply doubt or questioning in response to a statement.

In summary, intonation is crucial in English communication for conveying emotions, differentiating sentence types, highlighting important information, indicating continuation or completion, and managing conversational flow. Mastering intonation can significantly enhance both comprehension and expression in spoken English.

Task 1 Sample Analysis

Listen to the following sentences and practice the intonation used by the speaker.

1) When was the last time ↘ you experienced that?

2) Are you sure that isn't you every ↗ morning?

3) I for one, am feeling like that right now ↘!

4) Are you all with me ↗ so far?

5) Well, I might be wrong but isn't to "think positive" cliché over ↘ used ↗?

6) Wouldn't it be better to get into a daily ↘ habit? ↗

Task 2 Listen and Identify: Intonation

Listen to the following lecture about motivation affirmation provided by John P. Grima, an English lecturer at Tsinghua University. Identify the examples of intonation used by the speakers and practice after the recording.

Instructor: Hello class. Sometimes in life, work, or study, we come across a challenge that seems so difficult that we might feel like giving up. When was the last time [_____ intonation] you experienced that?

Student 1: That was me waking up this morning!

Student 2: Are you sure that isn't you every [_____ intonation] morning?

Students: [Laughter]

Student 3: I for one, am feeling like that right now [_____ intonation]!

Instructor: Well, everyone, you are not alone! It is human nature to experience a lack of motivation at times. So, if you're looking for a way to keep up your motivation and maintain a confident outlook, this session might help.

In this session, I will explain what motivation affirmations are, why they're important, and how to use them. Are you all with me [_____ intonation] so far?

Students: Yes.

Instructor: Excellent! Has anyone heard of motivation affirmations before [_____ intonation]?

Student 1: Are they statements that can help us remember positive things [_____ intonation]?

Instructor: Yes, these statements can help you maintain a confident mindset, remember the positive things about life, and stay motivated to achieve your objectives. These affirmations can take the form of visualizing a completed goal. For example, "I have achieved my goal of completing this speech." or a goal that you are working on, like "I will contribute my valuable ideas to this conference." They may even be quotes that remind you what you're working towards. Has anyone got a favorite motivational quote to share [_____ intonation]?

Student 2: I am a huge fan of Helen Keller's quote: "Optimism is the faith that leads to achievement."

Student 3: I personally prefer Steve Jobs' quote: "The only way to do great work is to love what you do."

Instructor: Absolutely! These statements encourage us to focus on the present situation through a positive lens.

Student 1: Well, I might be wrong but isn't to "think positive", cliché overused [_____ intonation]?

Instructor: Definitely, some clichés are overused but perhaps it helps go beyond this into deeper aspects of positivity and motivation. After all, research shows people tend to focus on negative things. This habit can have negative consequences, causing people to lose hope that they can lead a happy, fulfilling life. If people believed this, they would put less effort into trying to succeed.

Instructor: How might we best use motivation affirmations?

Student 2: I guess reciting them when we are lacking motivation might help [_____ intonation].

Student 1: Wouldn't it be better to get into a daily habit [_____ intonation]?

Instructor: These ideas are worth considering. Researchers suggest that incorporating motivation affirmations into your regular schedule might be an effective way to stay motivated and stay on track to achieve your goals. Let's keep up our motivation levels!

Supplementary Materials

1. A TED talk—"The Puzzle of Motivation"
2. A lecture—"Management: What Makes a Successful Manager"
3. A TED talk—"Everyday Leadership"

References

Catford, J. C. 2002. *A Practical Introduction to Phonetics*. Oxford: Oxford University Press.

Carnegie, D. 1990. *The Quick and Easy Way to Effective Speaking*. New York: Pocket Books.

Cook, A. 2017. *American Accent Training* (4th ed.). Hauppauge: Barron's.

Deterding, D. 2015. Segmentals. In M. Reed & J. M. Levis (Eds.), *The Handbook of English Pronunciation*. West Sussex: Wiley Blackwell.

Gilbert, J. B. 2012. *Clear Speech: Pronunciation and Listening Comprehension in North American English* (4th ed.). Cambridge: Cambridge University Press.

Gimson, A. C. 1964. *An Introduction to Pronunciation of English* (2nd ed.). London: Edward Arnold.

Hyland, K. 2005. *Metadiscourse*. London: Continuum.

Lucas, S. 2014. *The Art of Public Speaking*. New York: McGraw Hill.

Pennington, M. C. 1996. *Phonology in English Language Teaching: An International Approach*. New York: Routledge.

Roach, P. 2009. *English Phonetics and Phonology*. Cambridge: Cambridge University Press.

Rogers, H. 2000. *The Sounds of Language: An Introduction to Phonetics*. New York: Routledge.

Rothwell, J. D. 2017. *Practically Speaking* (2nd ed.). Oxford: Oxford University Press.

Siemund, P. 2013. *Varieties of English*. Cambridge: Cambridge University Press.

Swan, M. & Smith, B. 2001. *Learner English: A Teacher's Guide to Interference and Other Problems* (2nd ed.). Cambridge: Cambridge University Press.

Tabrizi, A. & Abbasi, S. 2016. The effect of oral summary of short stories on Iranian intermediate EFL learners' vocabulary learning: With a focus on gender. *International Journal of English Linguistics*, 6(6): 129–137.

Yoshida, M. T. 2016. *Beyond Repeat After Me: Teaching Pronunciation to English Learners*. Alexandria: TESOL International Association.

教师服务

感谢您选用清华大学出版社的教材！为了更好地服务教学，我们为授课教师提供本学科重点教材信息及样书，请您扫码获取。

❯❯ 最新书目

扫码获取 2024 **外语类**重点教材信息

❯❯ 样书赠送

教师扫码即可获取样书